By the Sea

COLOR BY NUMBER

COLORING BOOK

George Toufexis

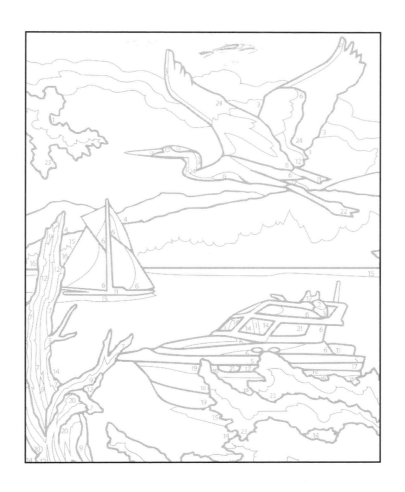

DOVER PUBLICATIONS, INC.
MINEOLA, NEW YORK

This coloring collection features forty-six expertly drawn full-page illustrations of beautiful seaside scenes for you to color. Each illustration is shown in color on the inside covers. You can duplicate these images simply by following this color guide or choose your own colors for a more personal touch. As part of Dover's *Creative Haven* series for the experienced colorist, each highly detailed image features picturesque scenes of boats, lighthouses, palm trees, seabirds, and other maritime sights. Plus, perforated, unbacked pages offer you the opportunity to experiment with any media you like, and make displaying your artwork easy!

Bibliographical Note

By the Sea Color by Number Coloring Book is a new work, first published
by Dover Publications, Inc., in 2020.

International Standard Book Number

ISBN-13: 978-0-486-84046-8
ISBN-10: 0-486-84046-8

Manufactured in the United States by LSC Communications
84046803
www.doverpublications.com

4 6 8 10 9 7 5 3

2020

INTRODUCTION

The artwork in this book is based on 24 colors (white is blank and shade is black or any darker color) that approximate a standard set of color pencils or fine markers. You can certainly use more colors if you wish, but 24 will allow you to fully color the artwork presented here.

Color number "0" is called "shade." Black or any dark color is used to darken the color above, below, or next to it by "overlaying," which is a technique of softly applying a dark color over an existing color. You will see that the "0" is usually very close to the color number it's supposed to darken. It's best to use a light touch when shading with black over a lighter color. If you are using markers, add the shade with a darker color pencil.

White is represented as a blank space with the exception of spaces that are too small or thin to house a number. In those cases, following the immediate color pattern will yield the best results.

TIPS AND TECHNIQUES

Because of the level of detail in this book, it is best to use hard color pencils, allowing for a thinner line.

A good way to start is to moderately (lightly, softly) apply the lightest and darkest colors first. As you add the mid range colors you will be able judge how intense the lights and darks need to be. (You can go over your colors several times.)

Although the color spaces have outlines separating them, it is better to let the colors "bleed" into each other for a softer appearance. This applies particularly to fur, clothing, background trees, and clouds. Exceptions are rocks, buildings, and most objects' outside edges.

You will notice that there are various line thicknesses in the artwork. A good way to make your artwork "pop" is to go over some of the heavier gray outlines with black or a dark color. Remember that the further away an object is, the lighter the outline should be. For example, where color is required for cloud shadows, it is best to use a light touch so that they look more distant.

There are several birds and other animals depicted in many of the images and because of their small size, numbers cannot fit in their spaces. You can therefore use whatever color you prefer in these instances.

Remember also to turn your artwork so that your hand can comfortably move in the appropriate direction for the types of strokes you wish to use.

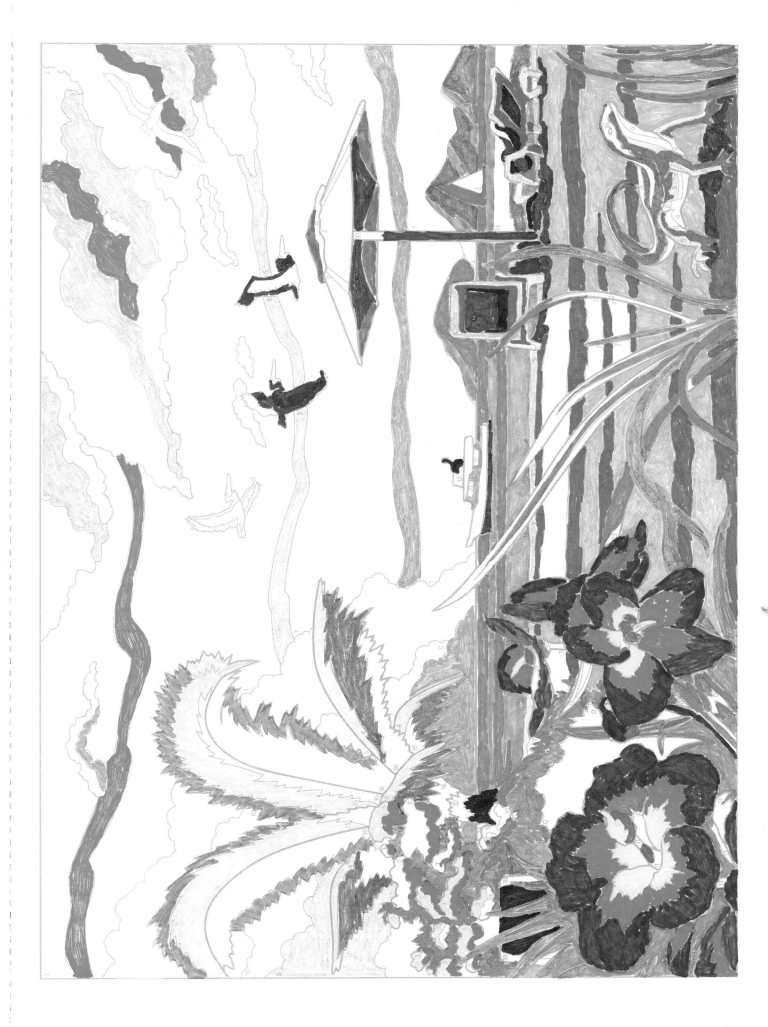

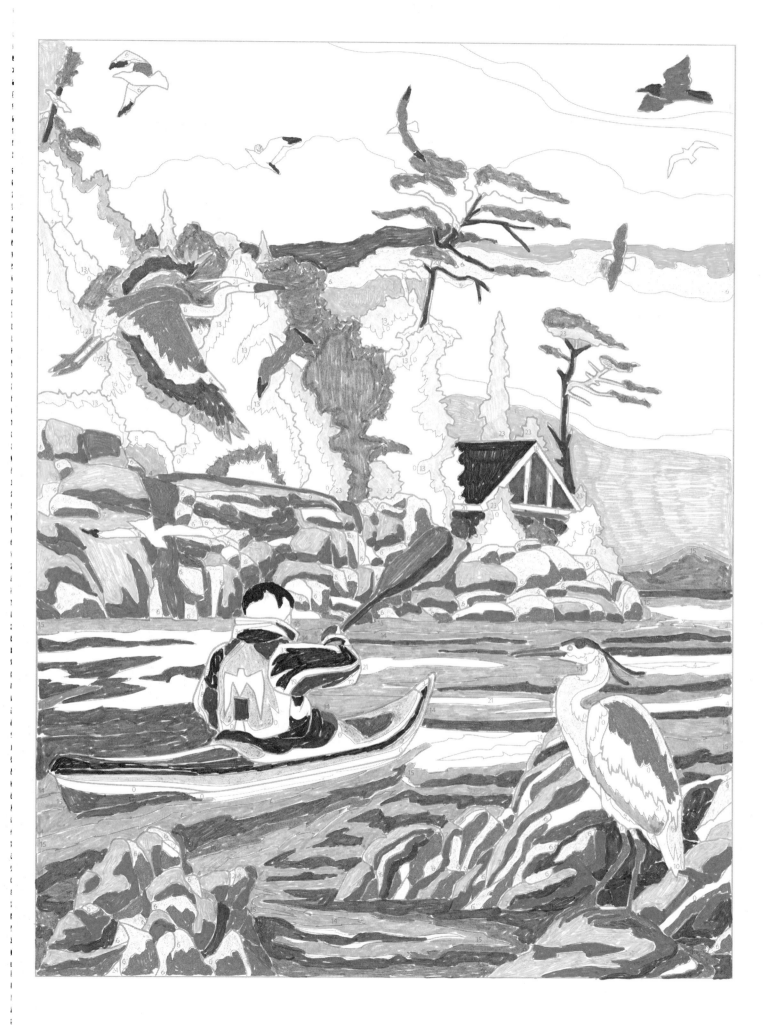

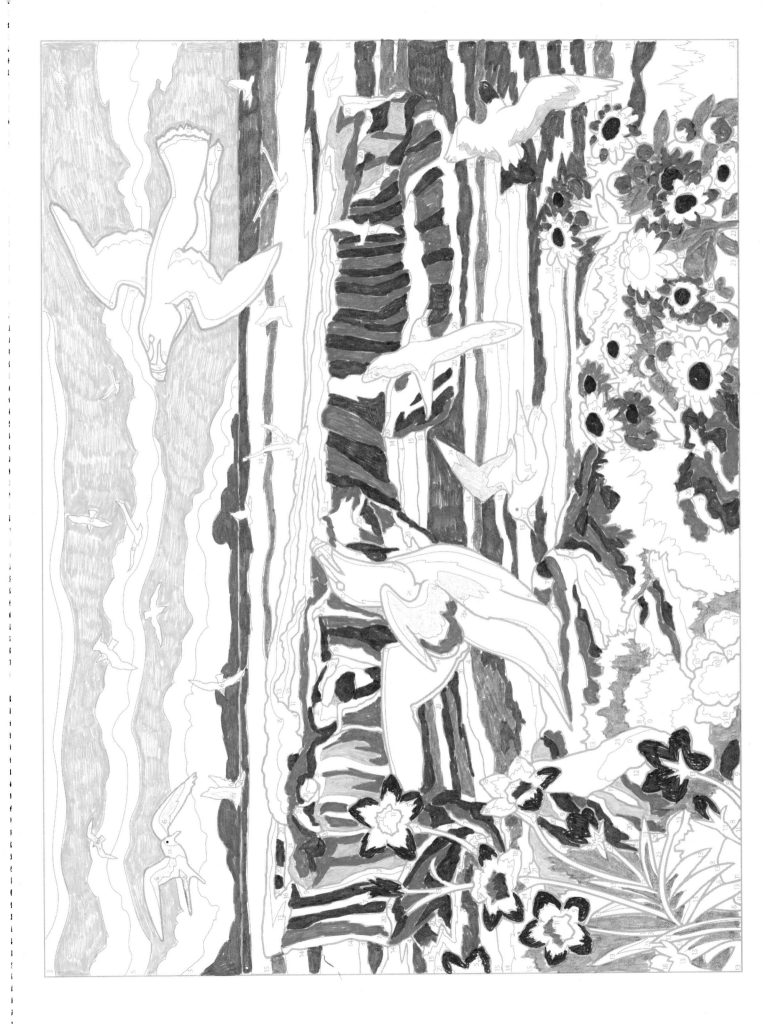

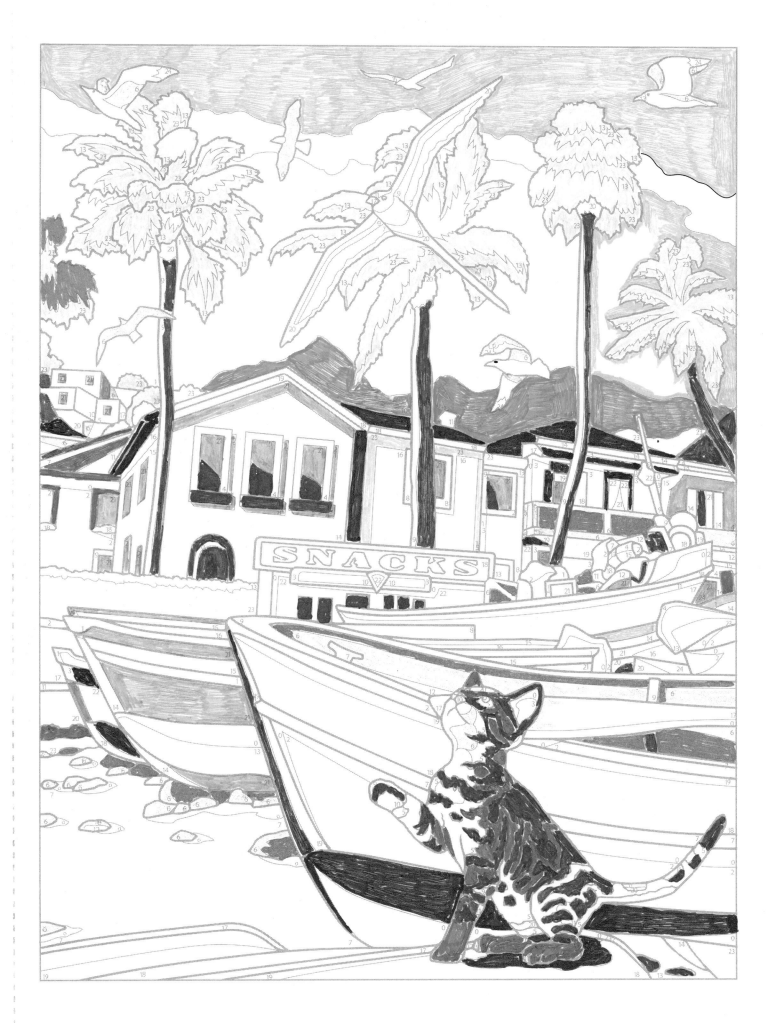

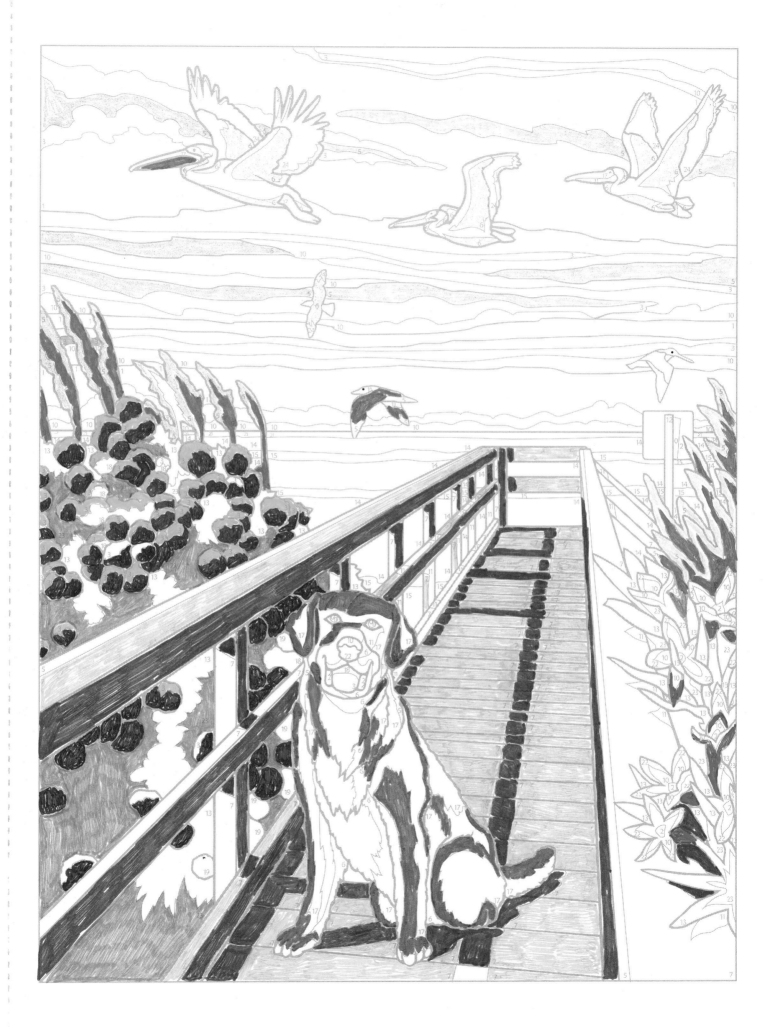

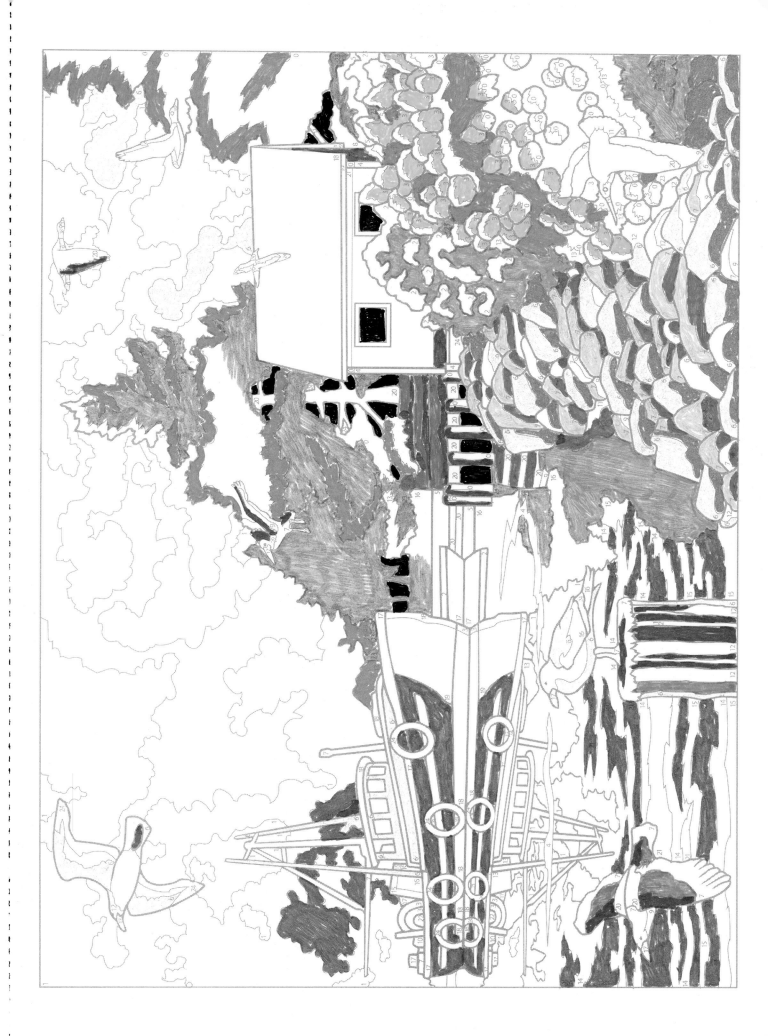

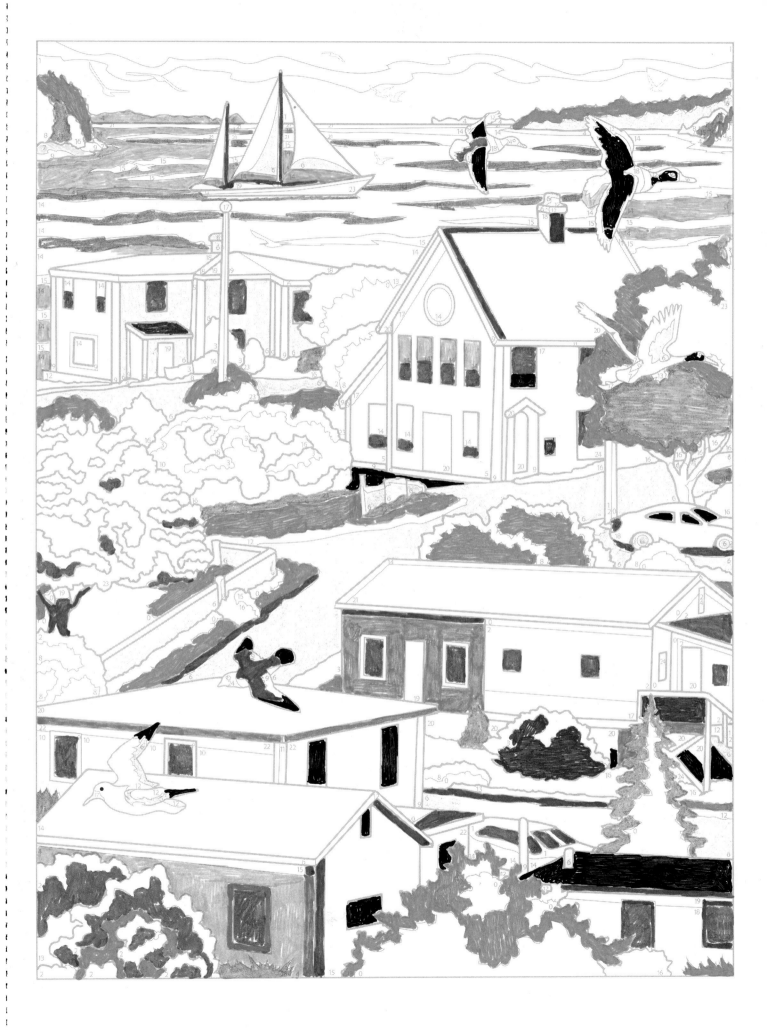

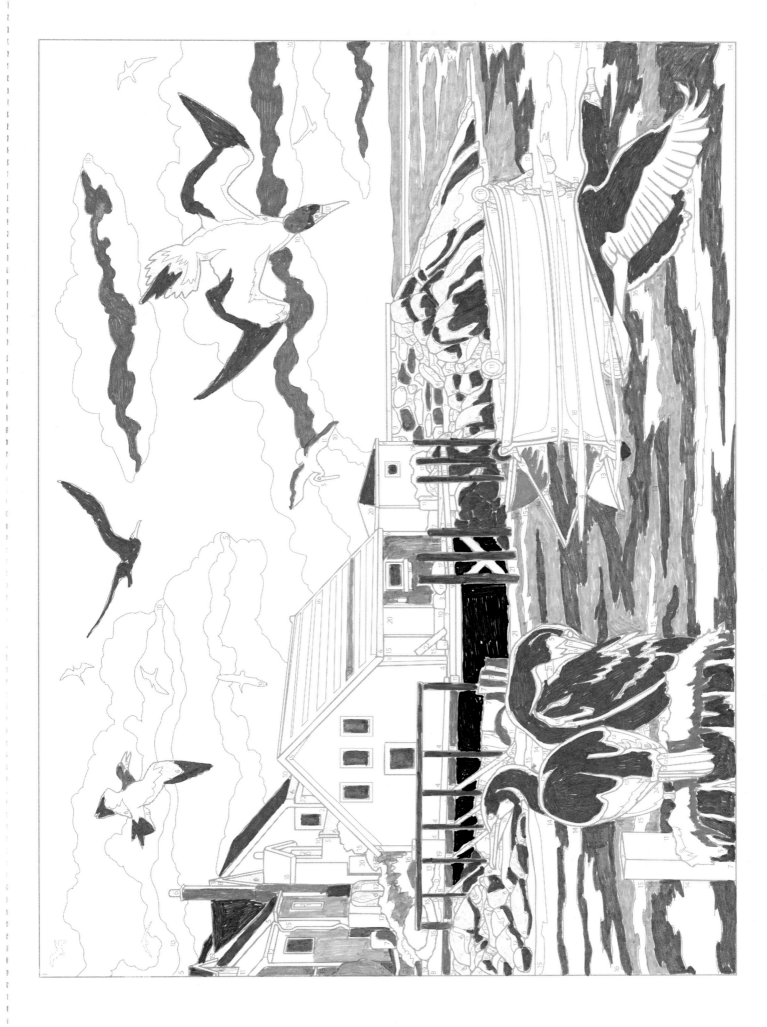

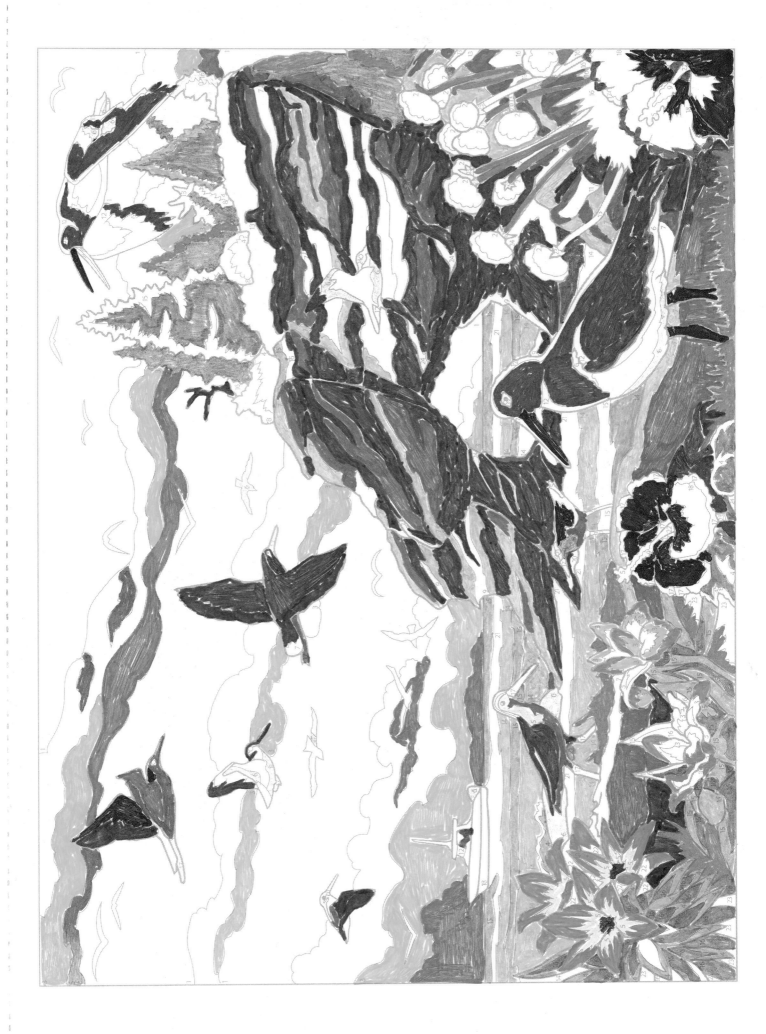

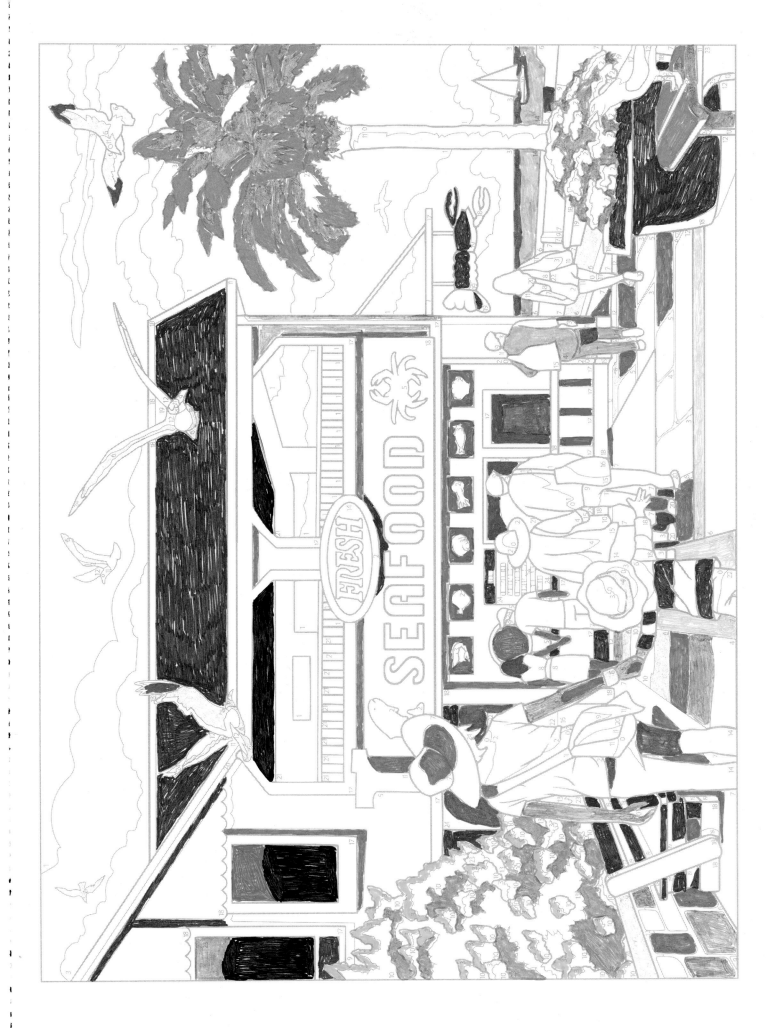

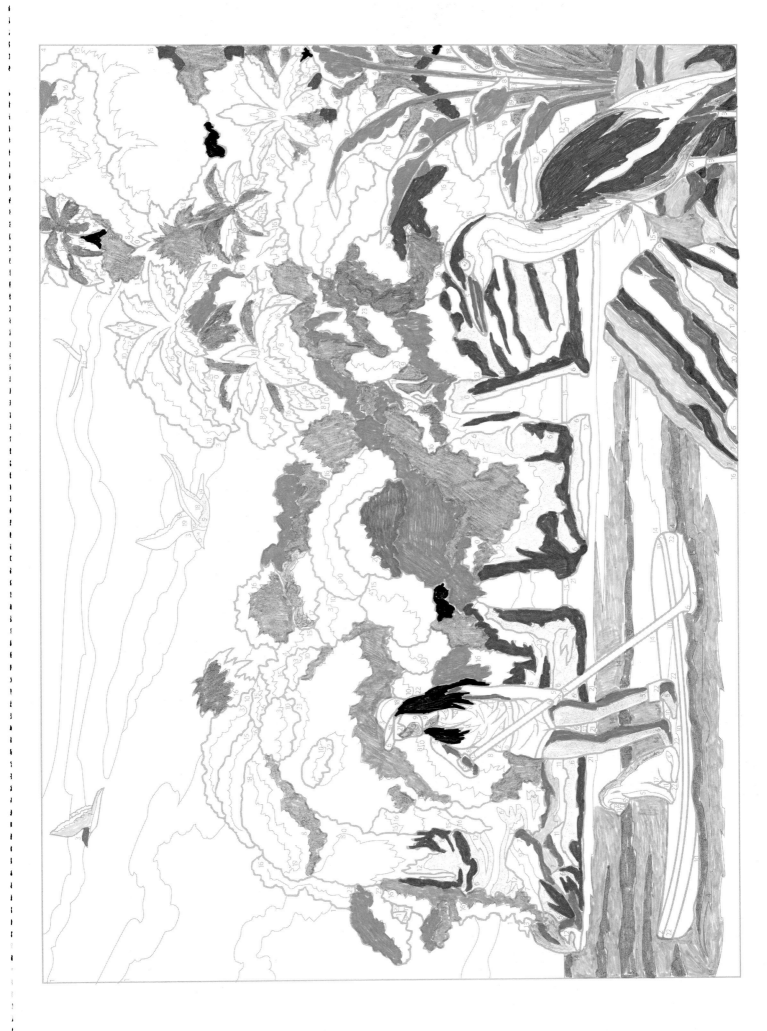

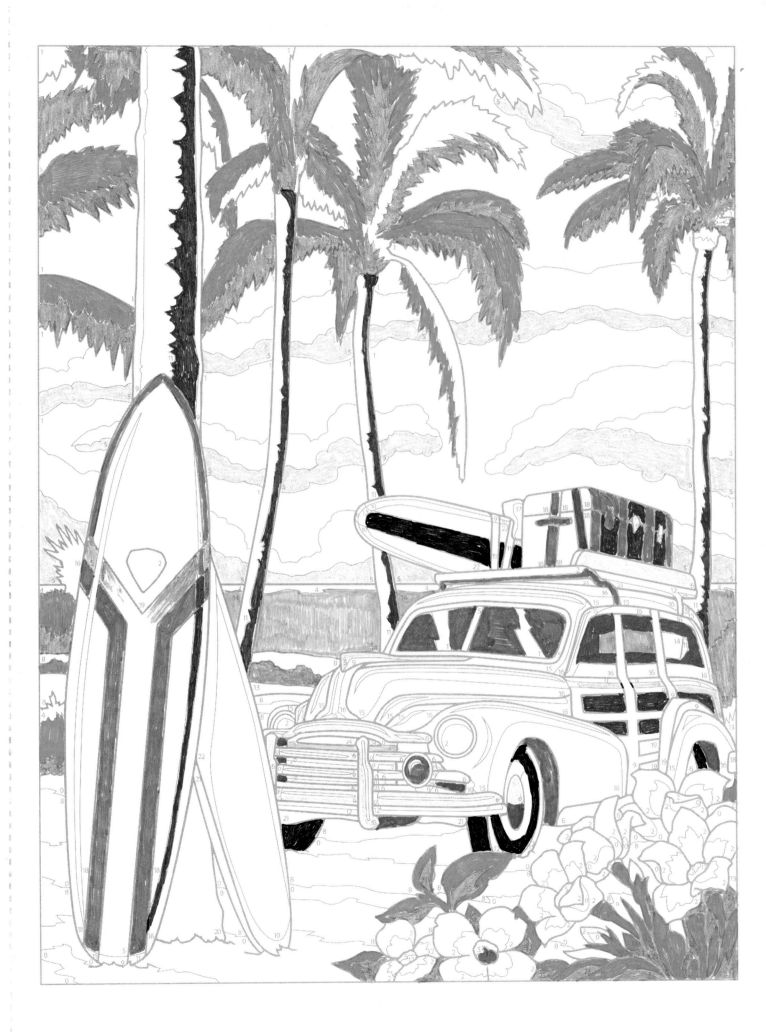

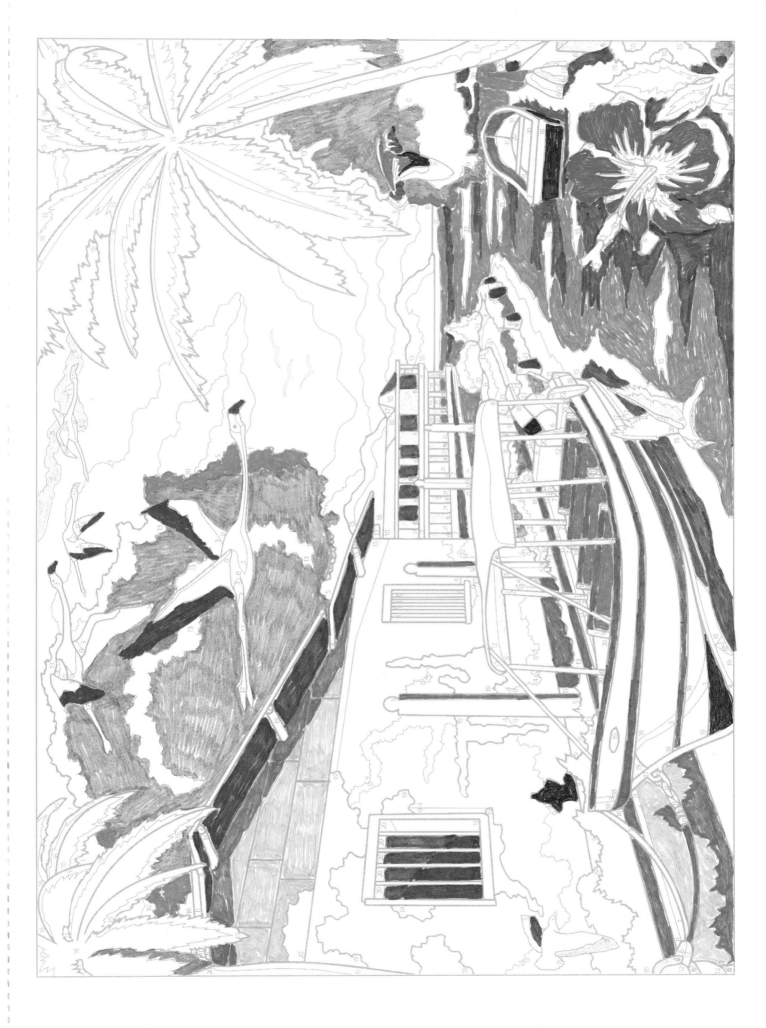

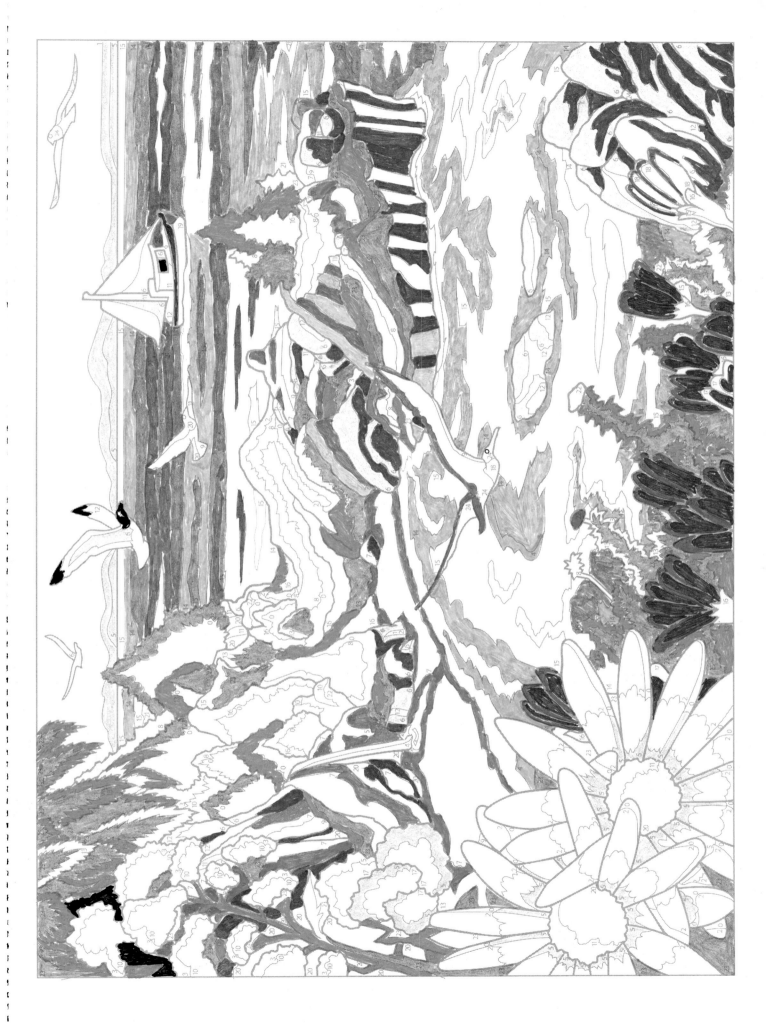

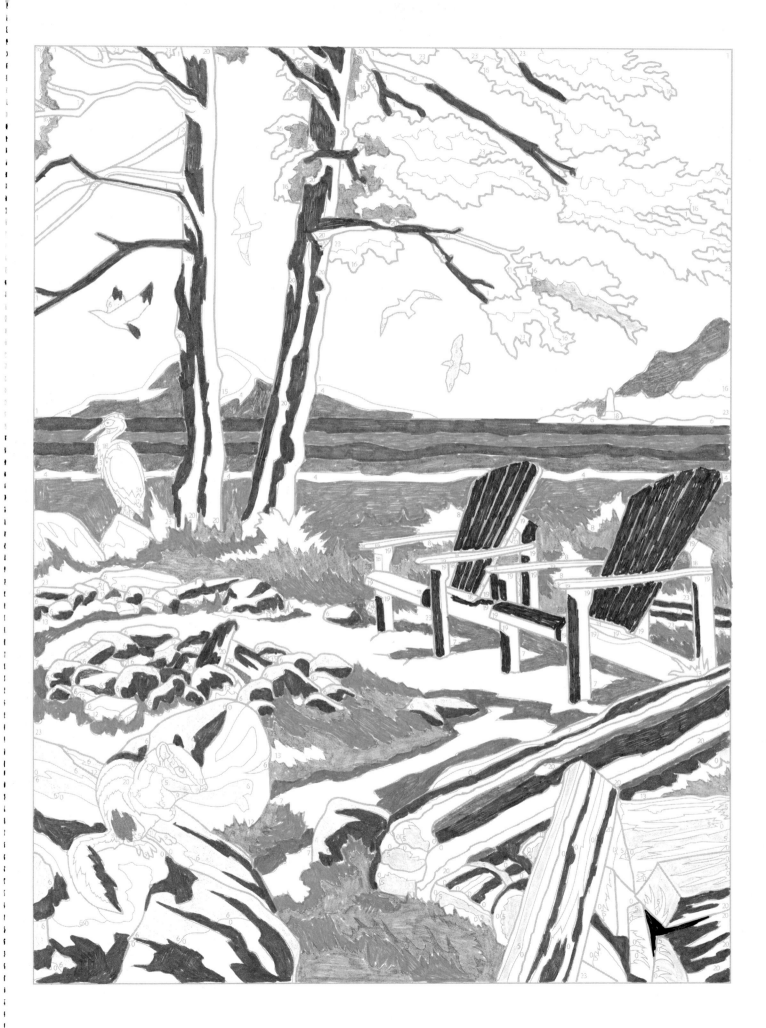

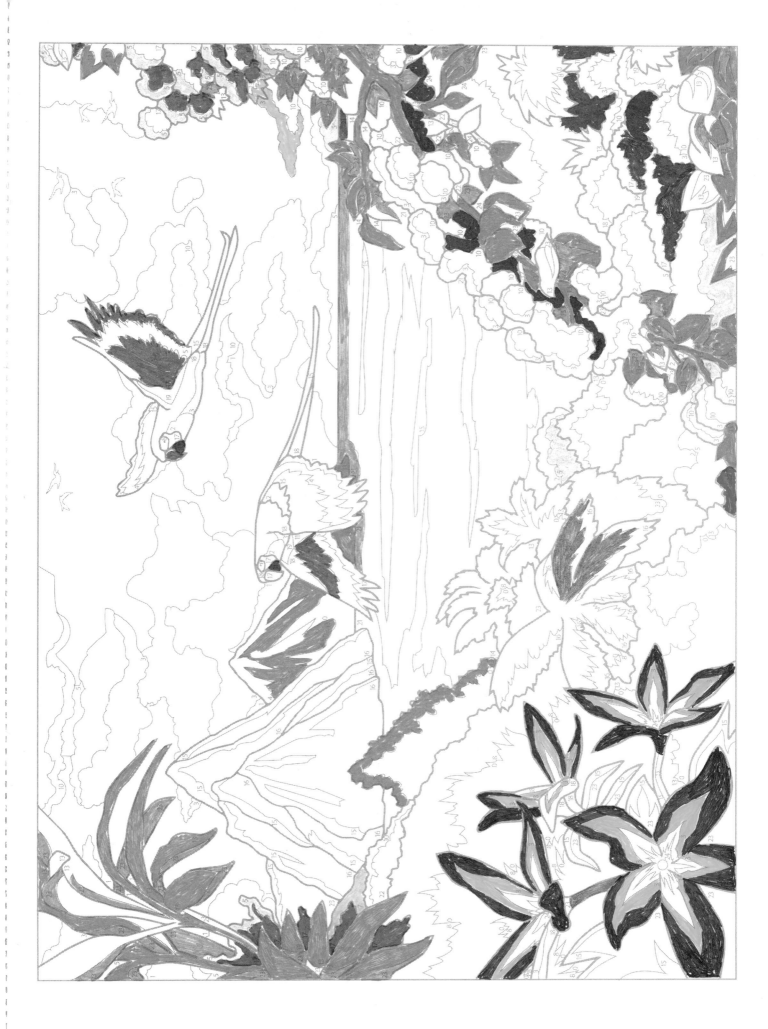

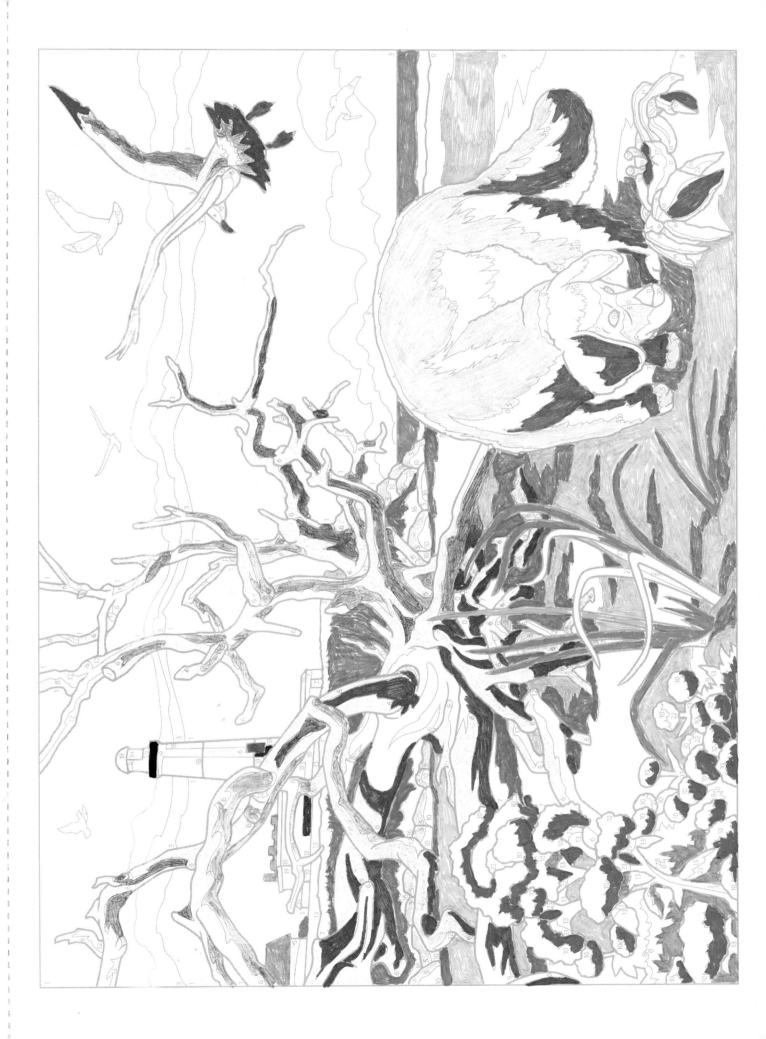

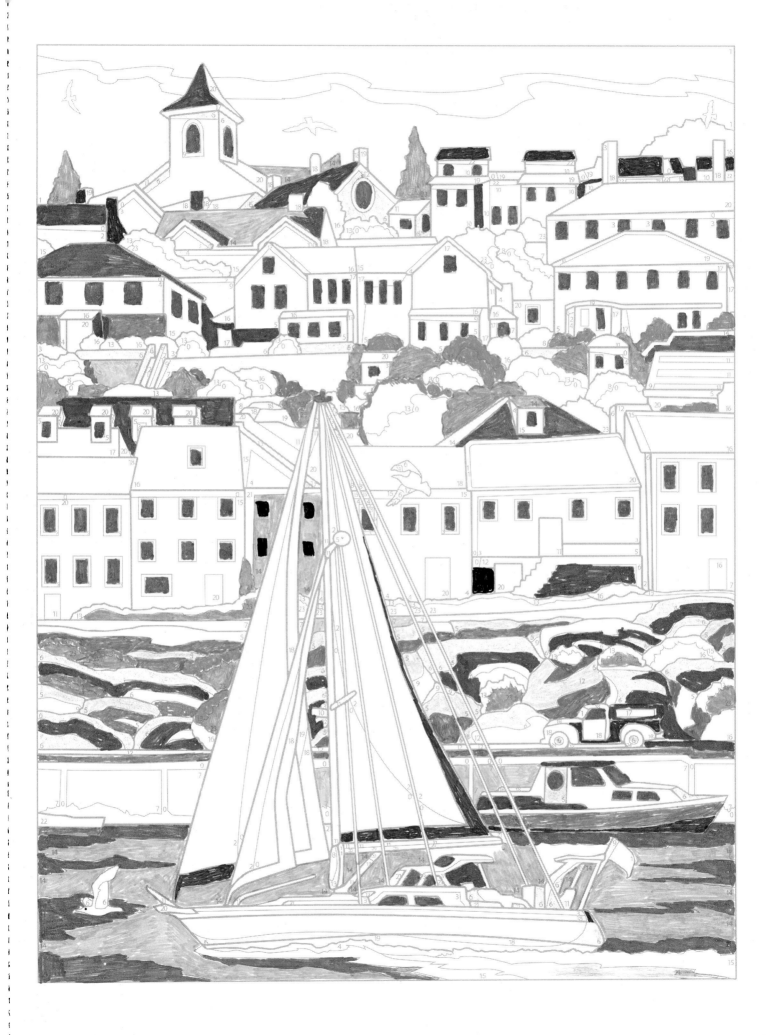

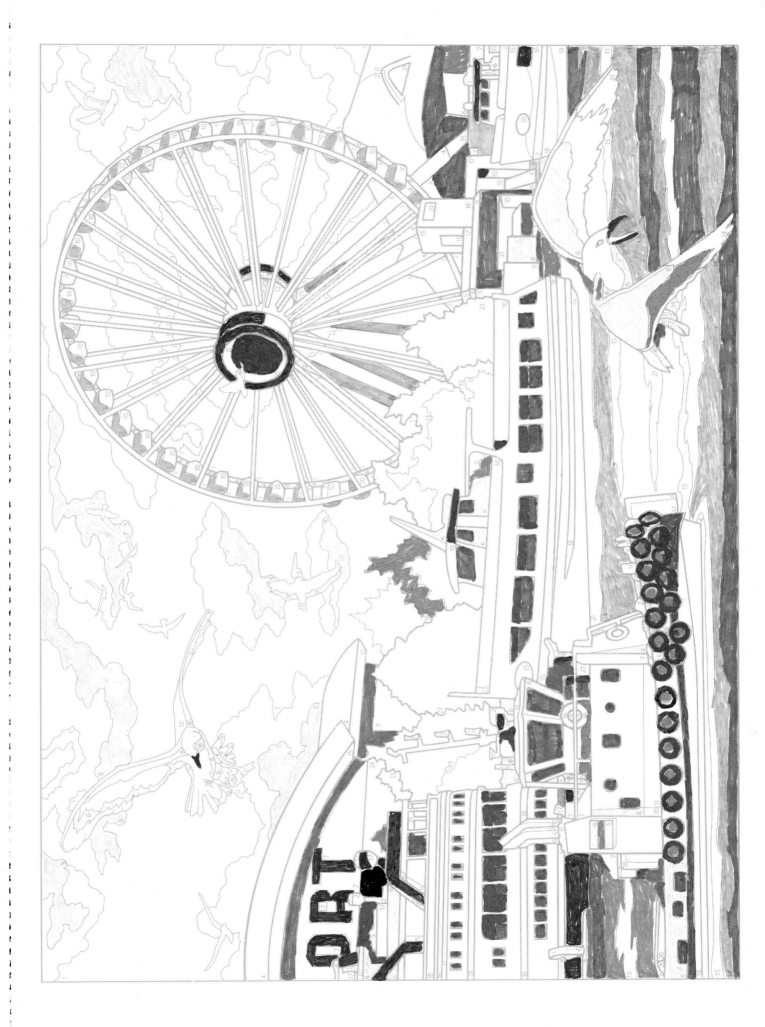

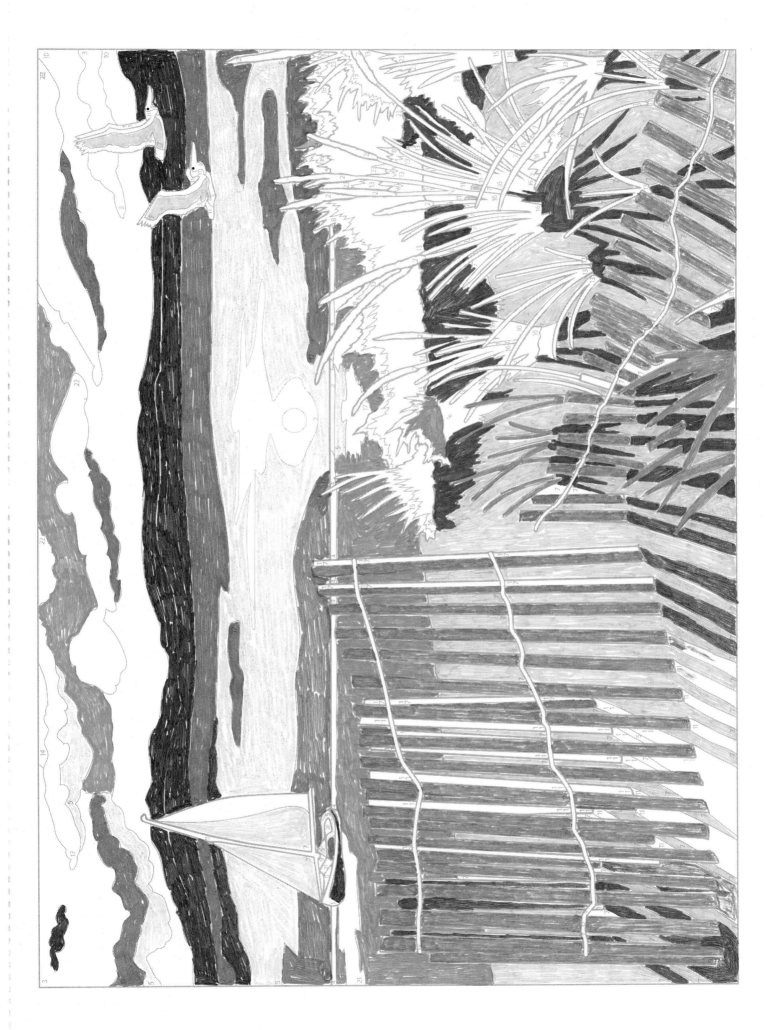

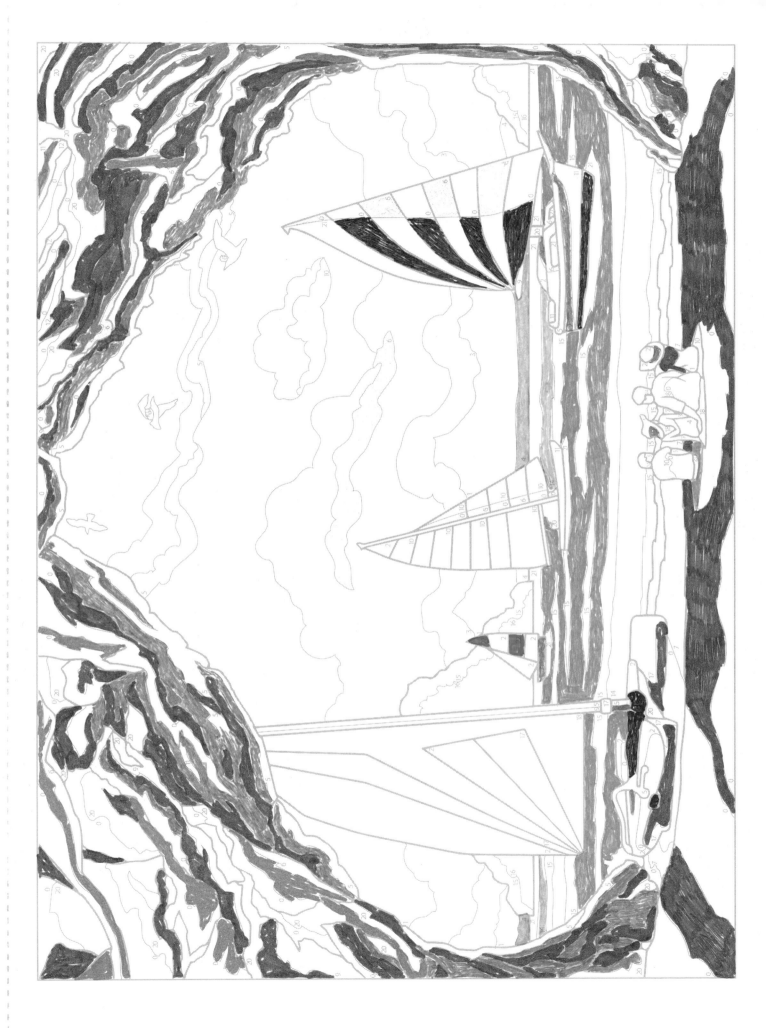

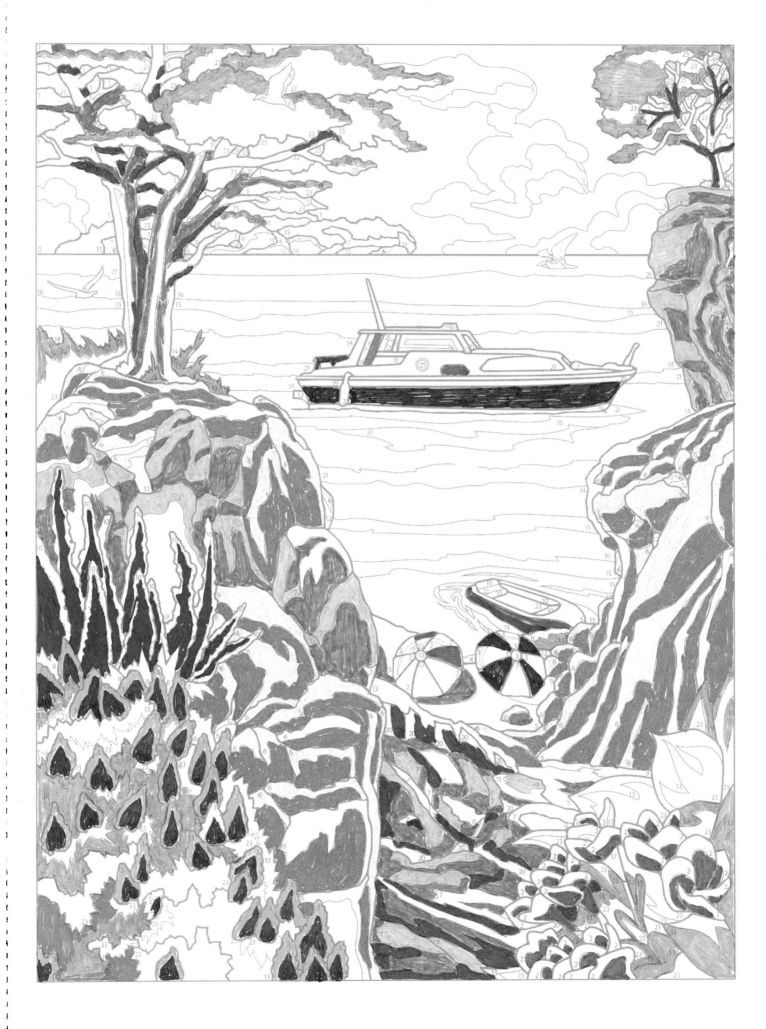

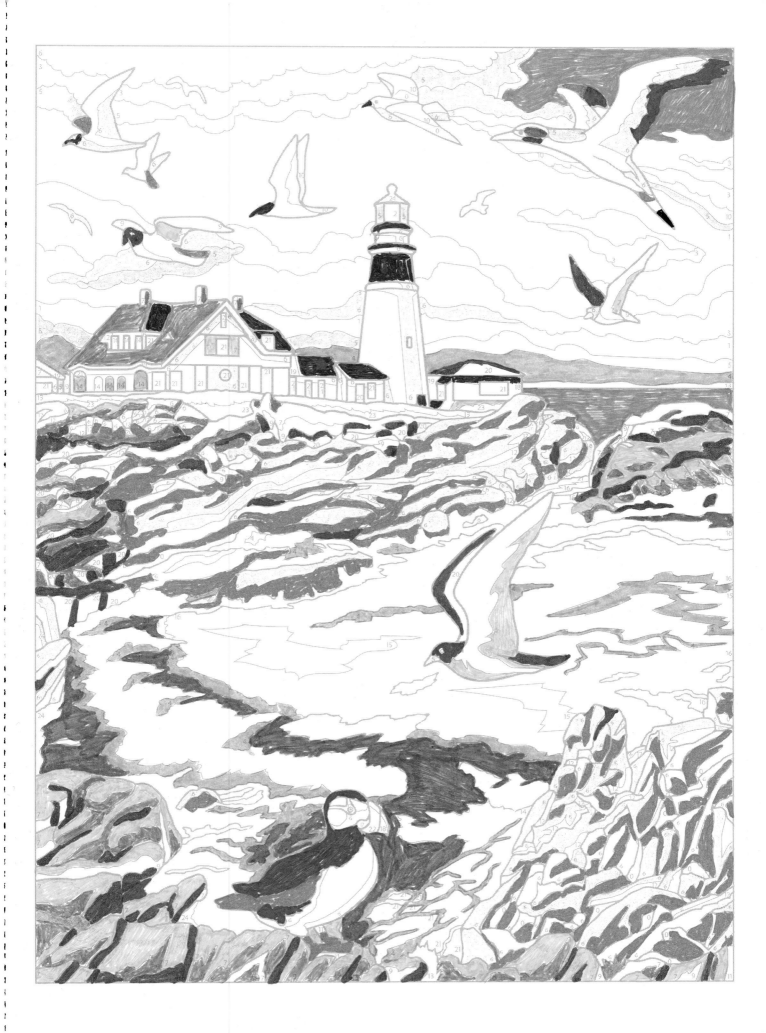

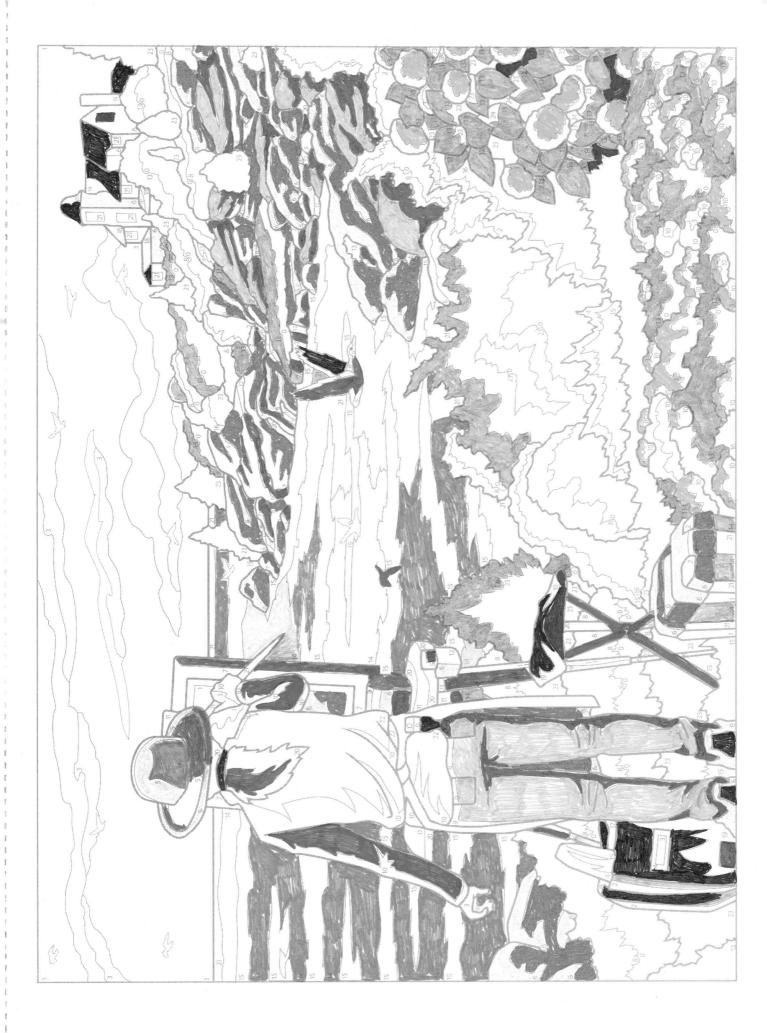

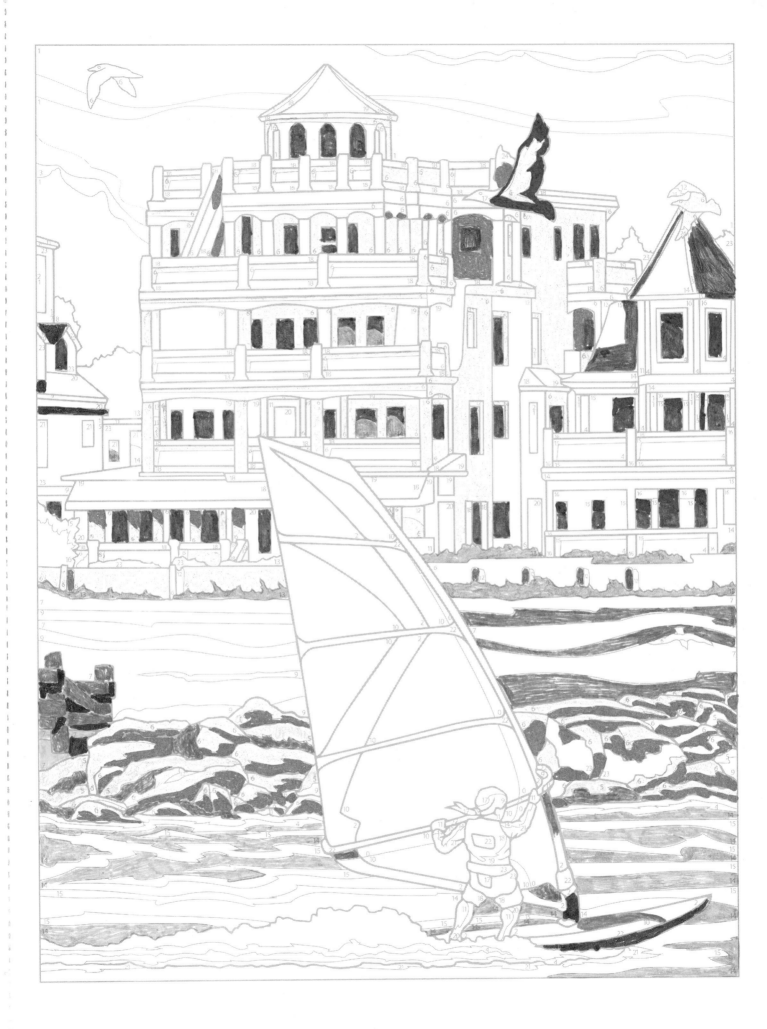

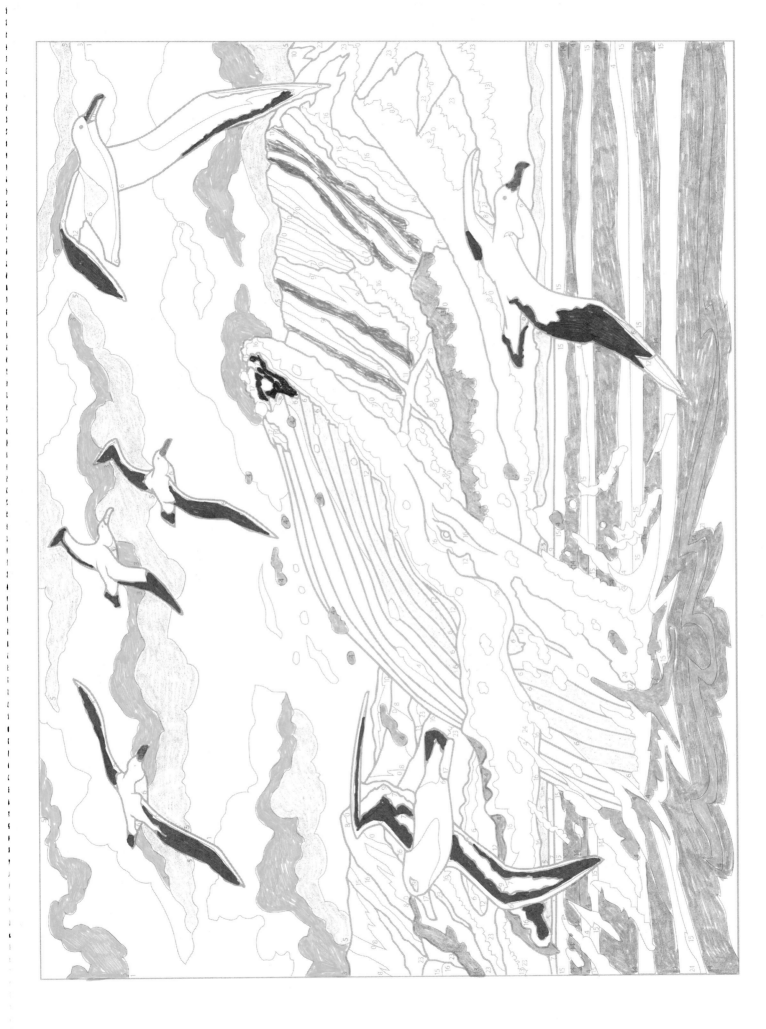

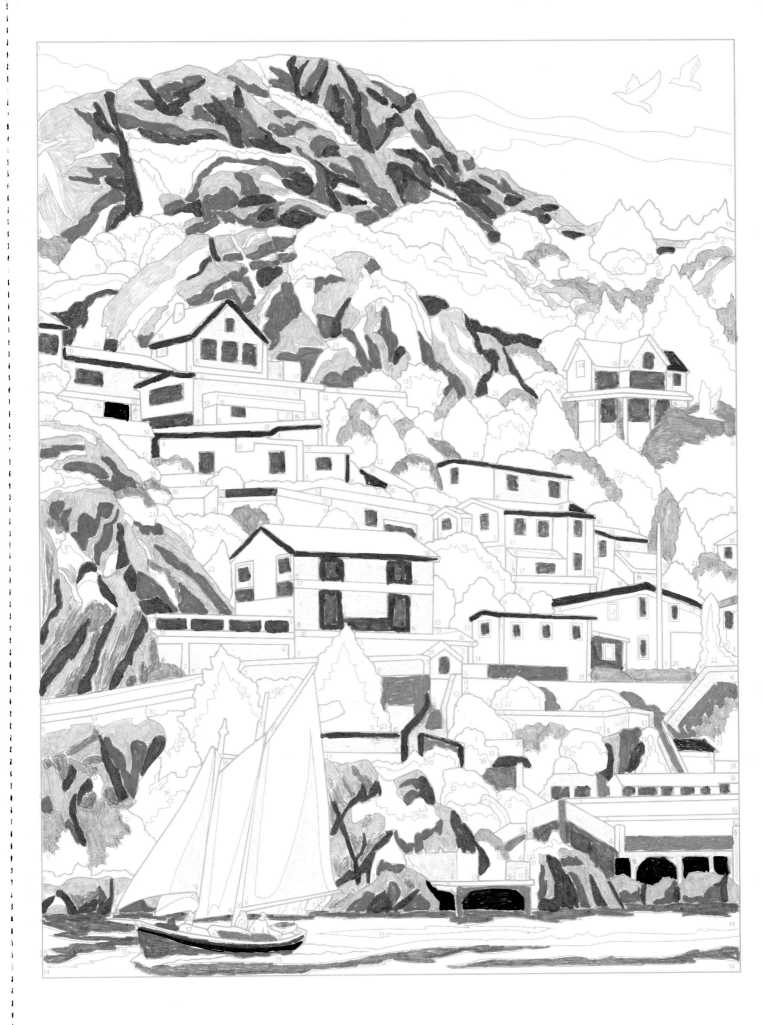

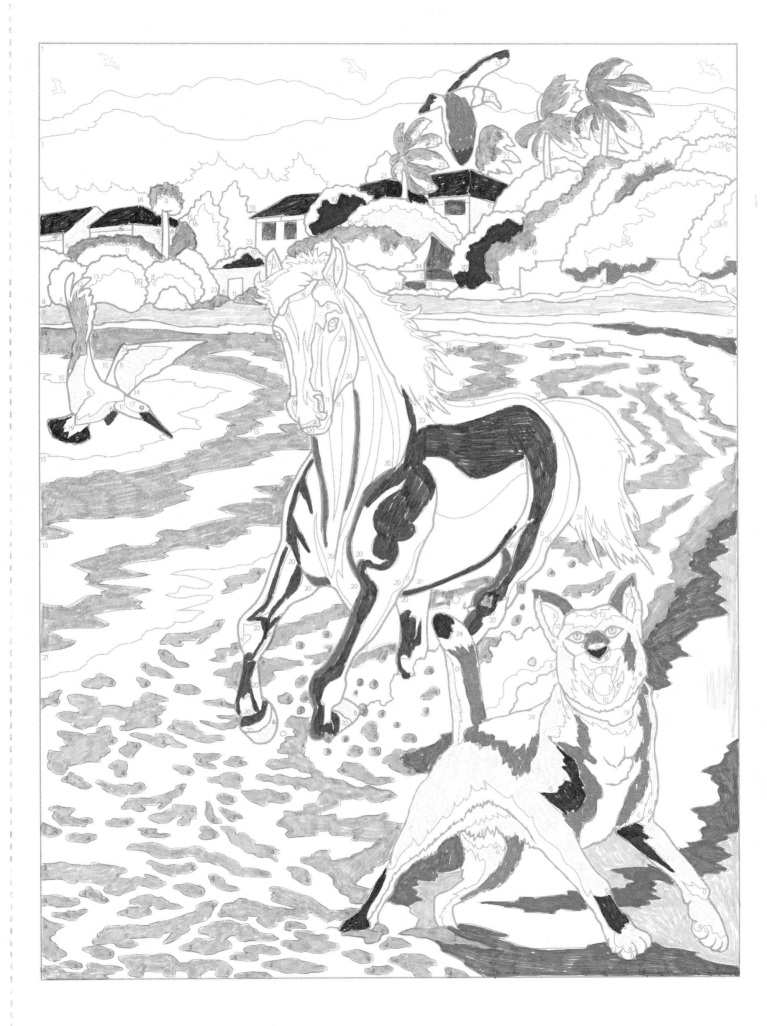

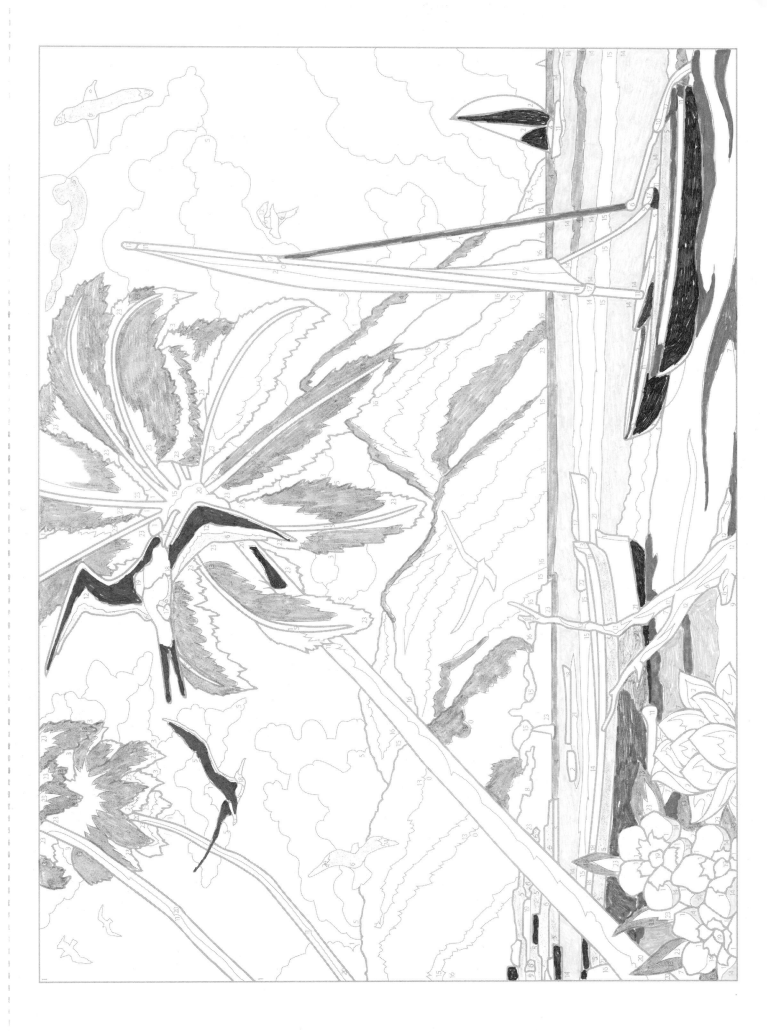

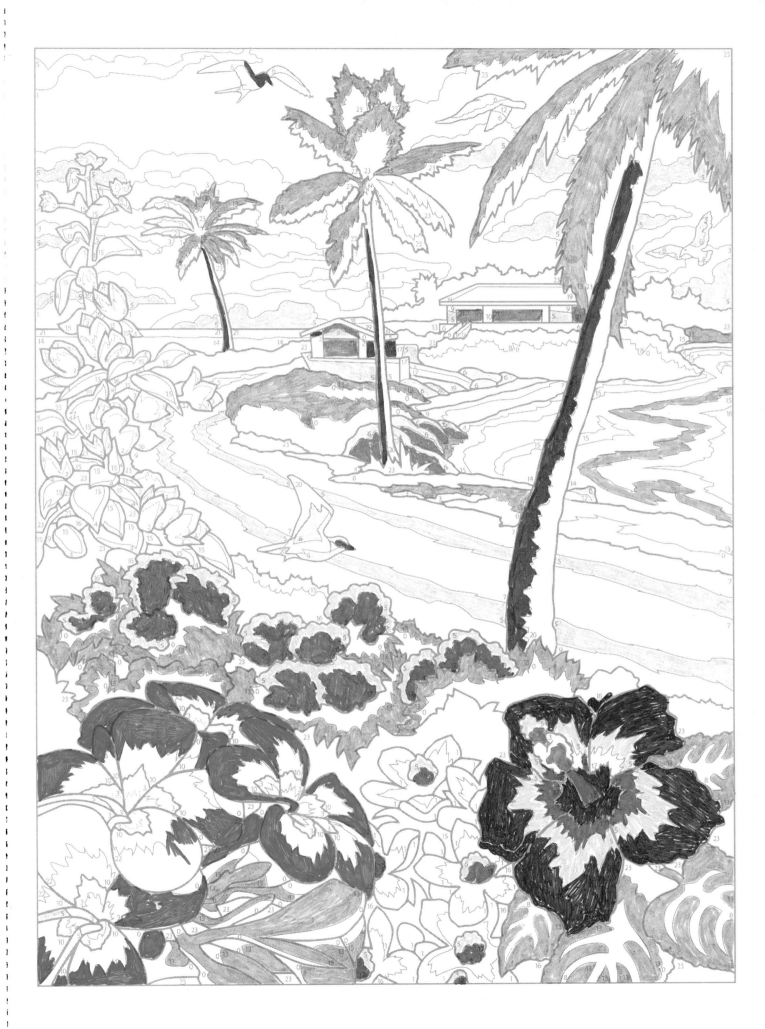

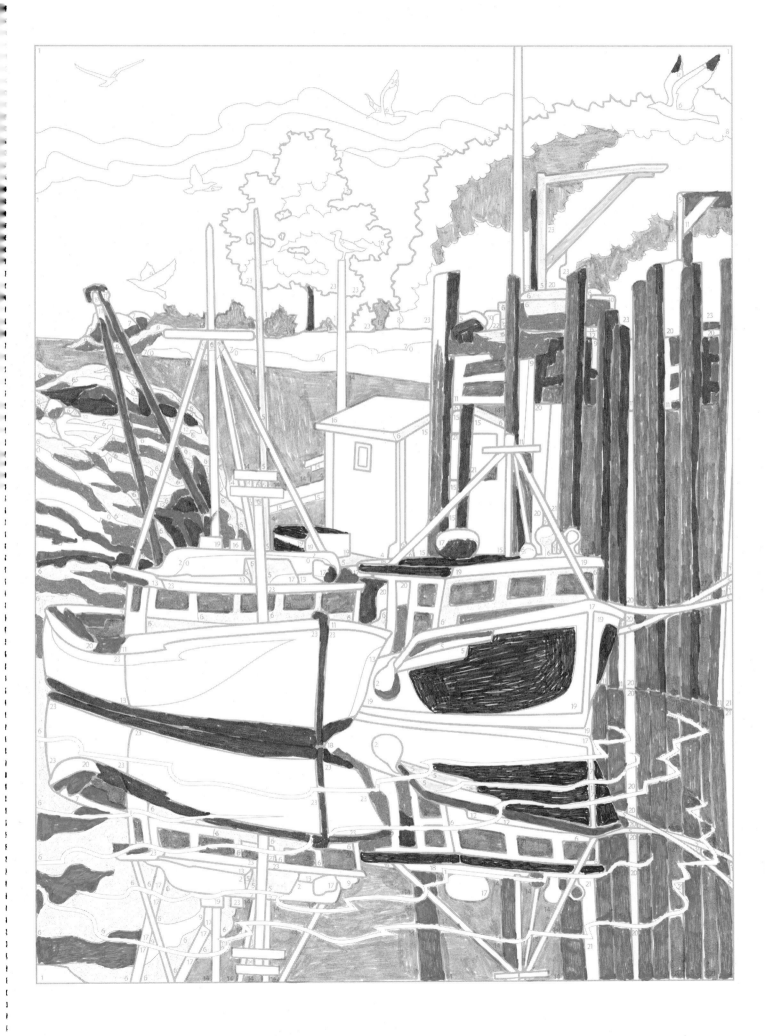

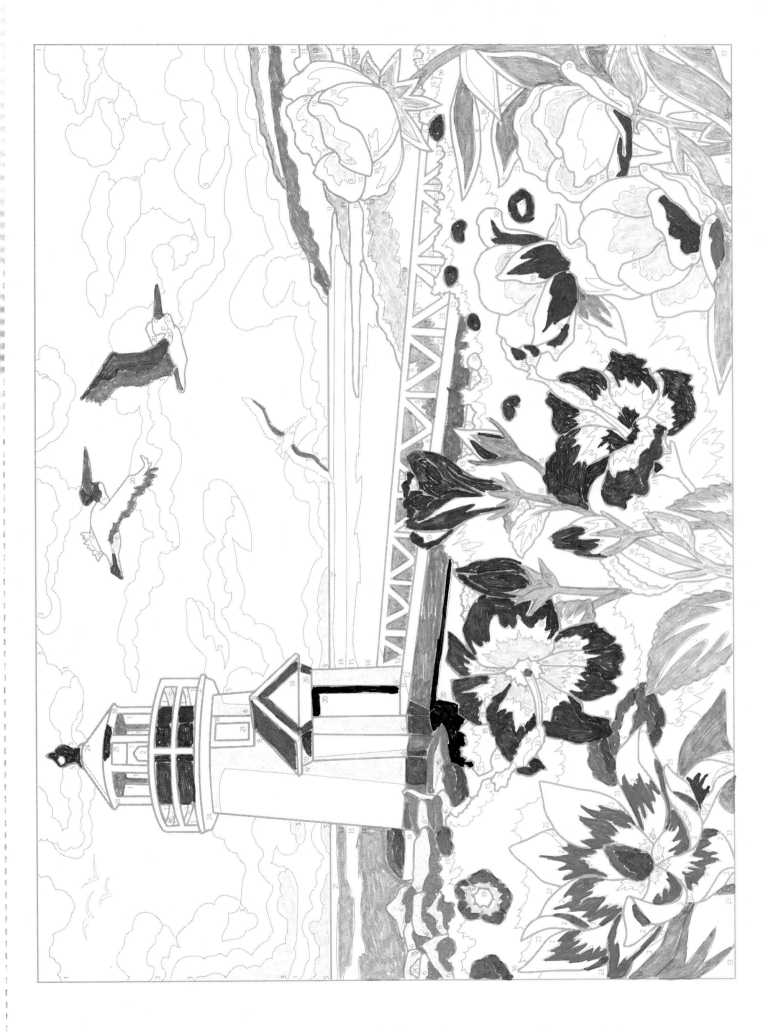

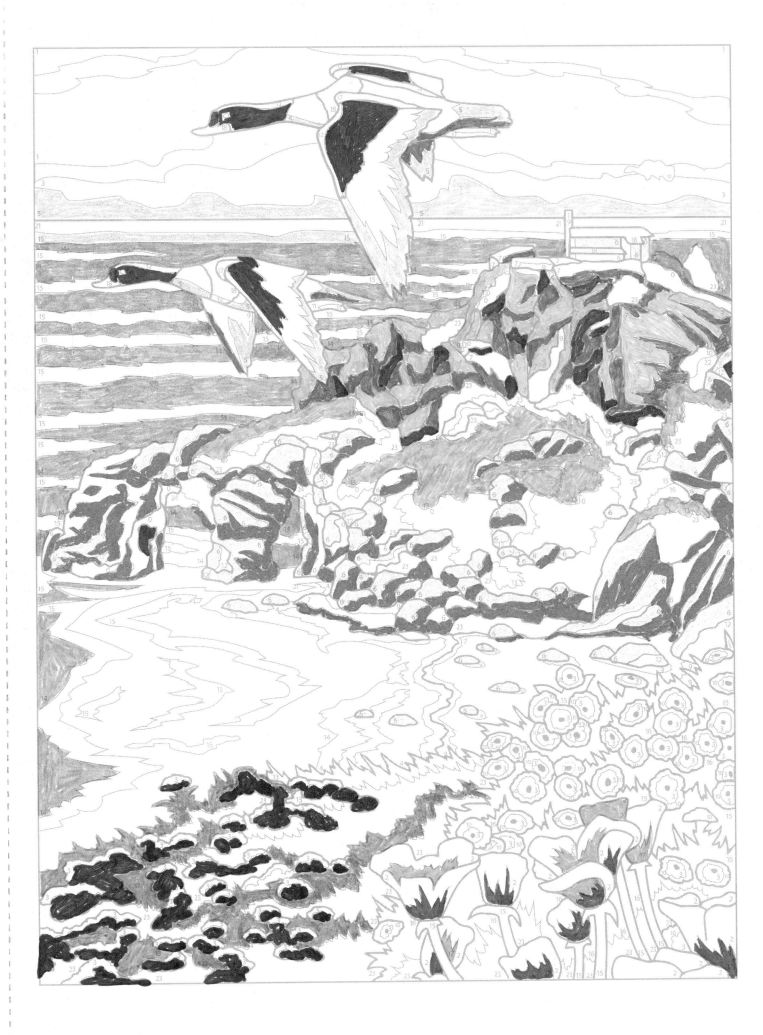

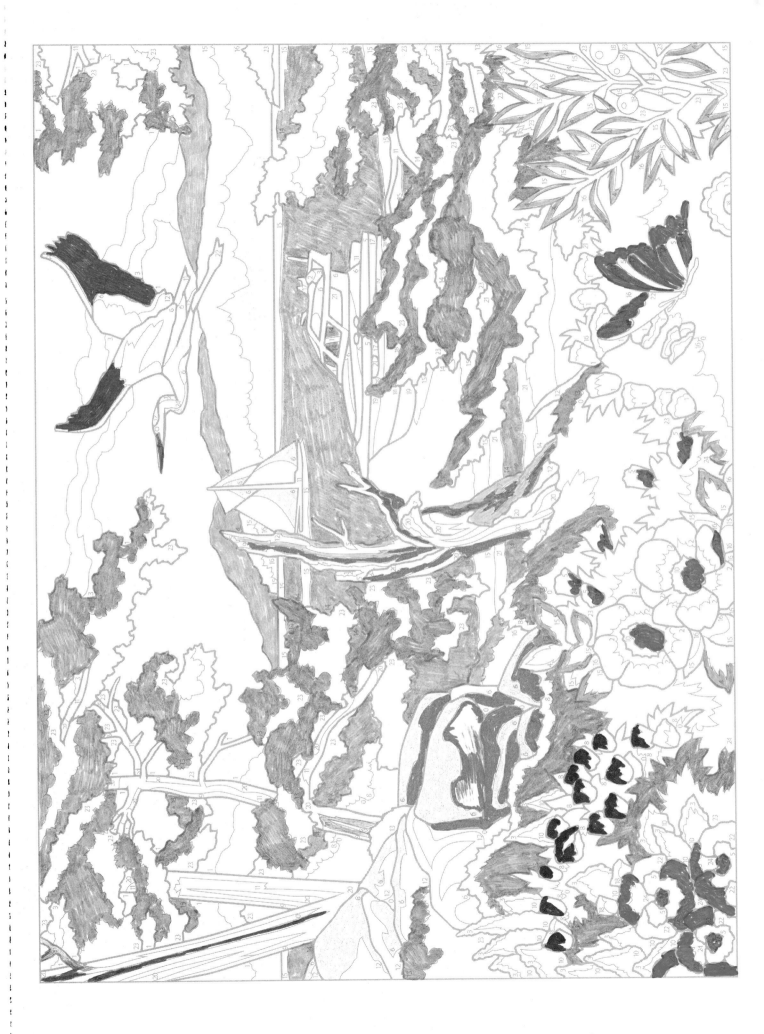

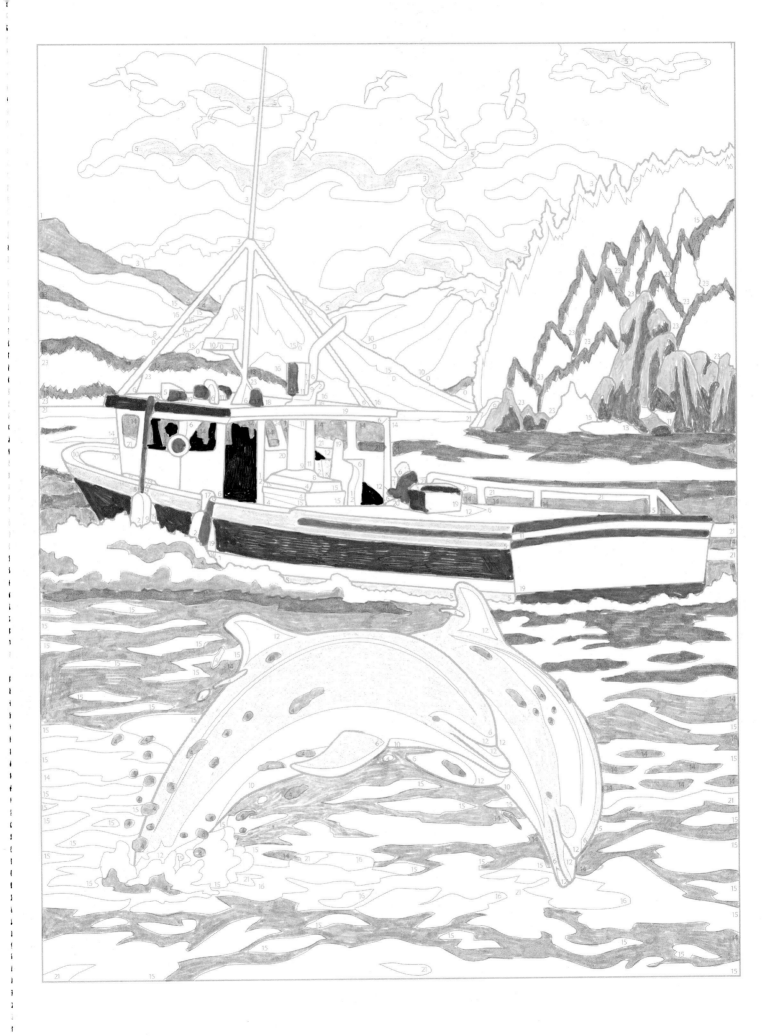

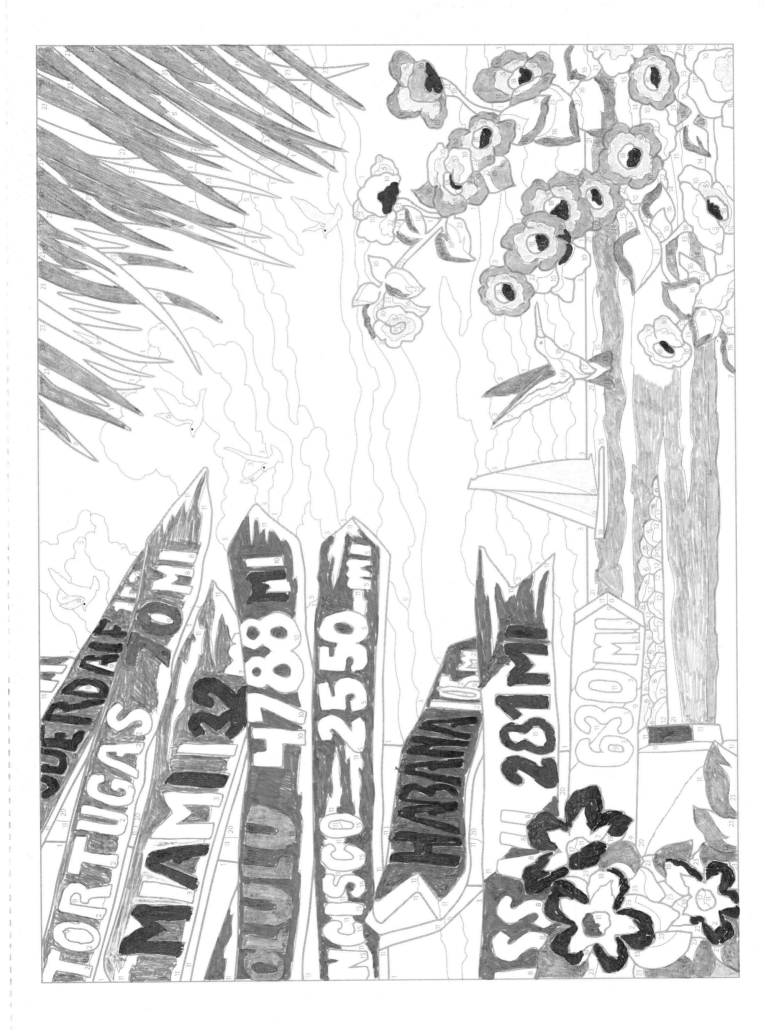

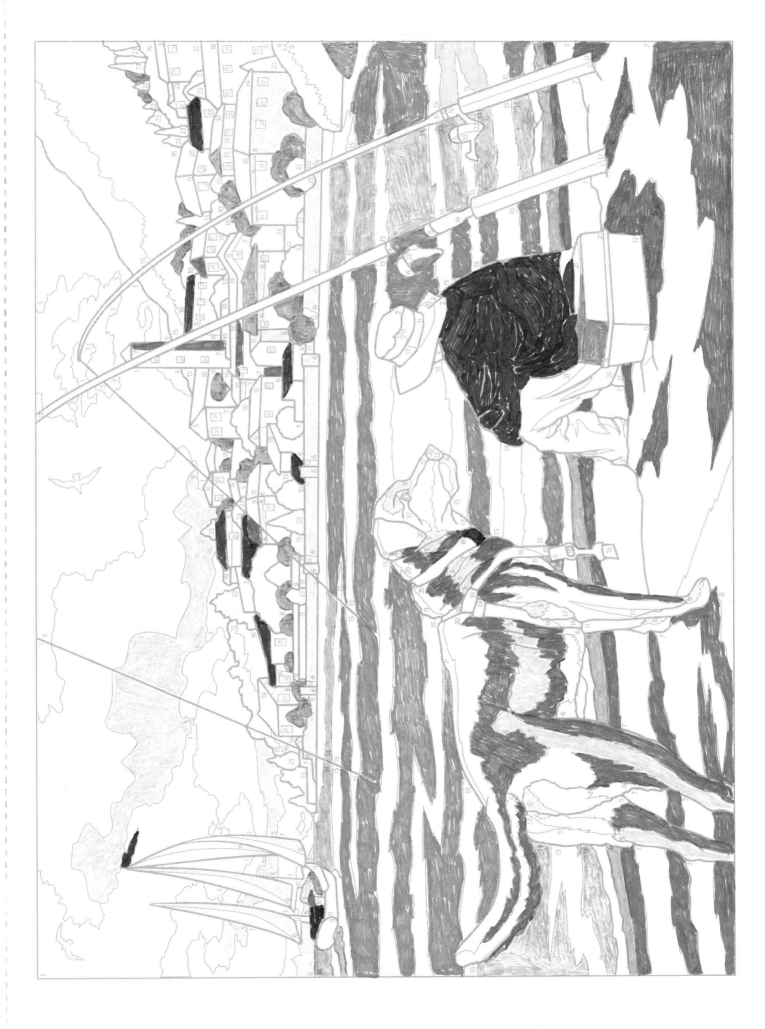

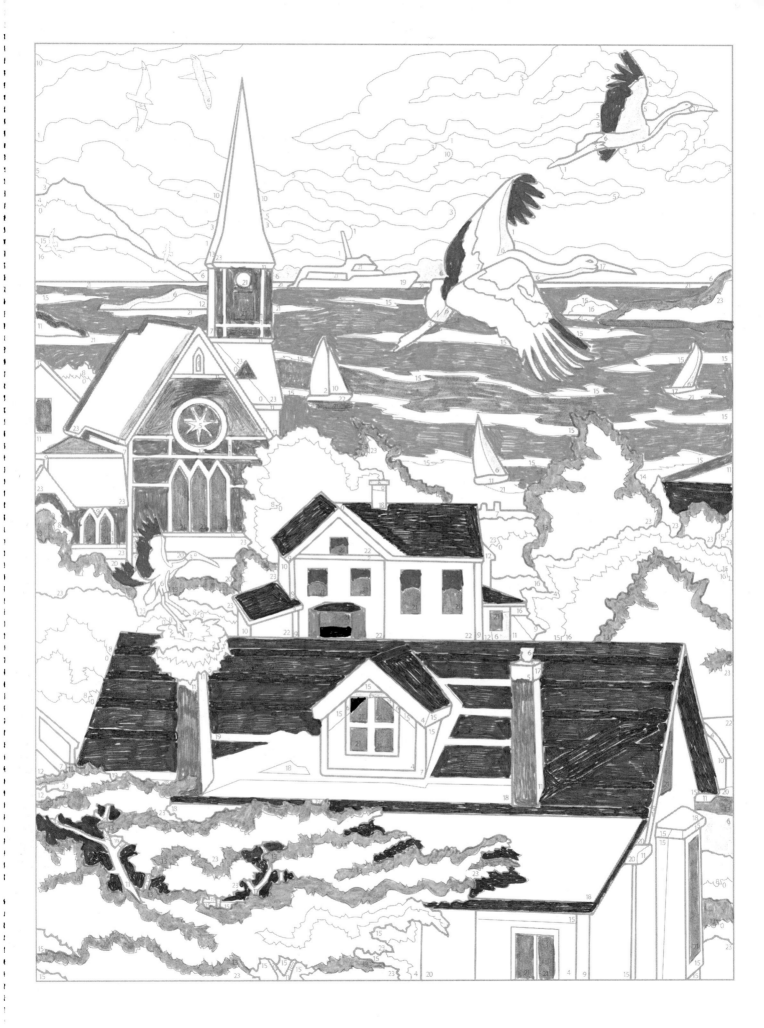

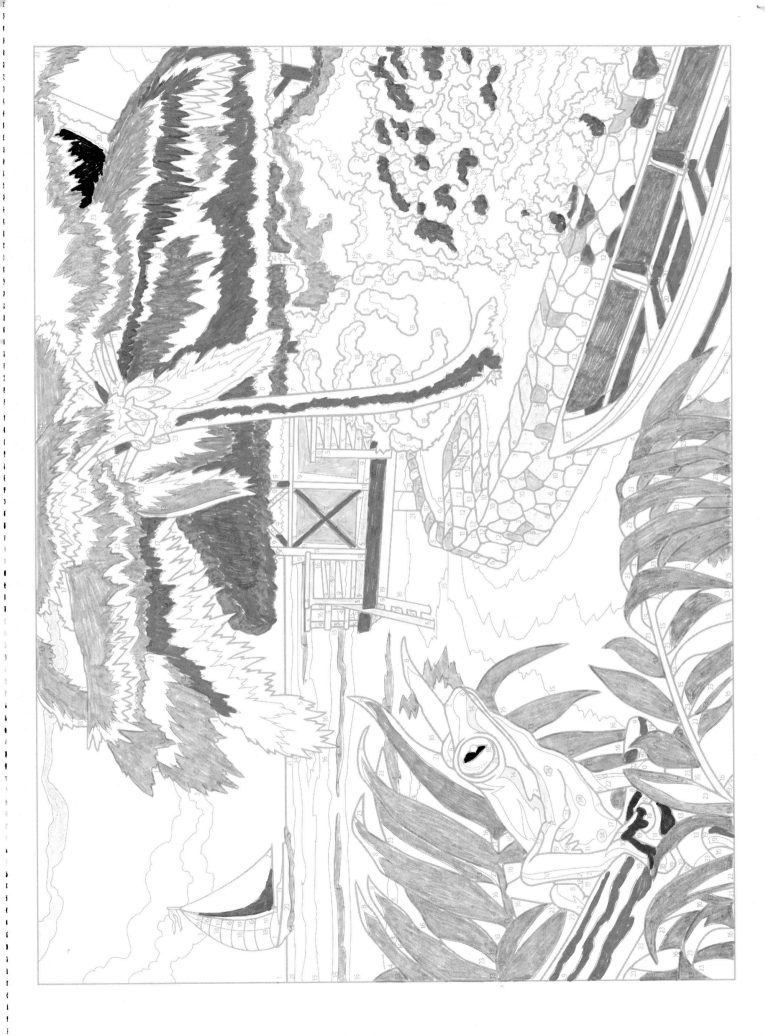

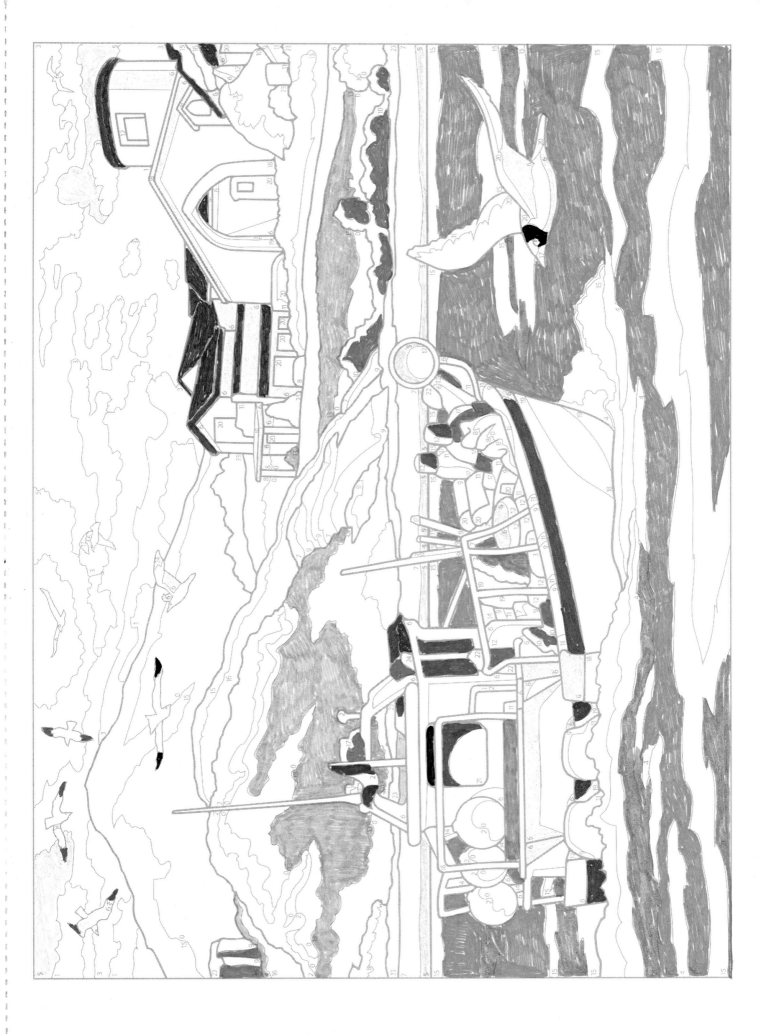

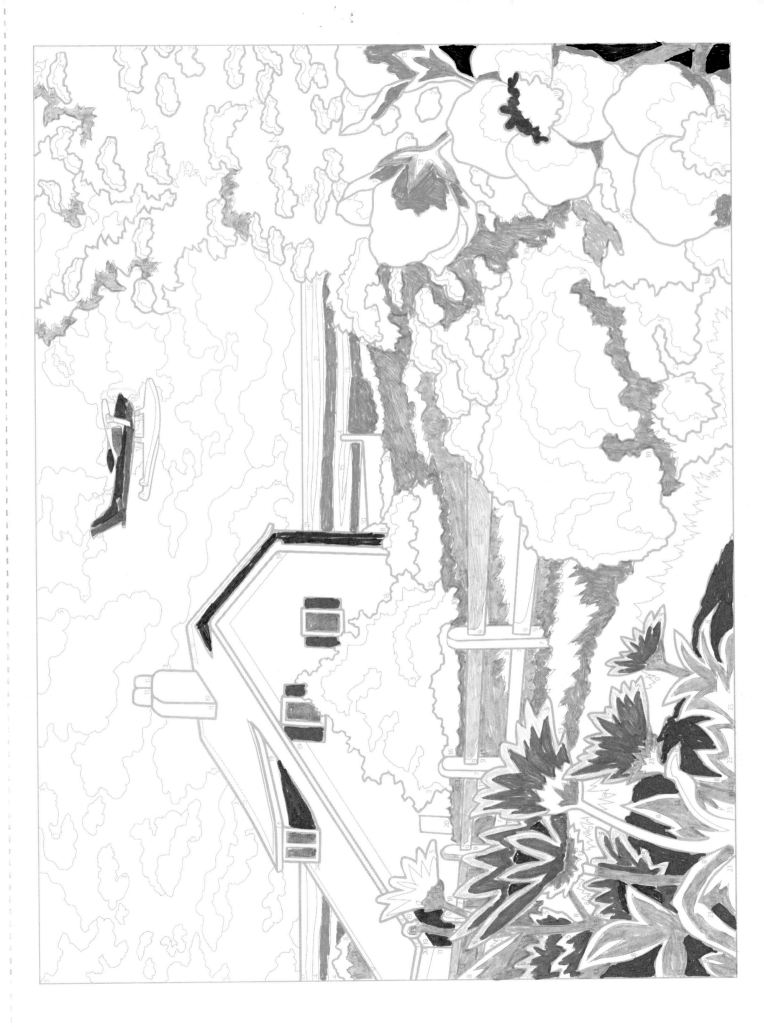

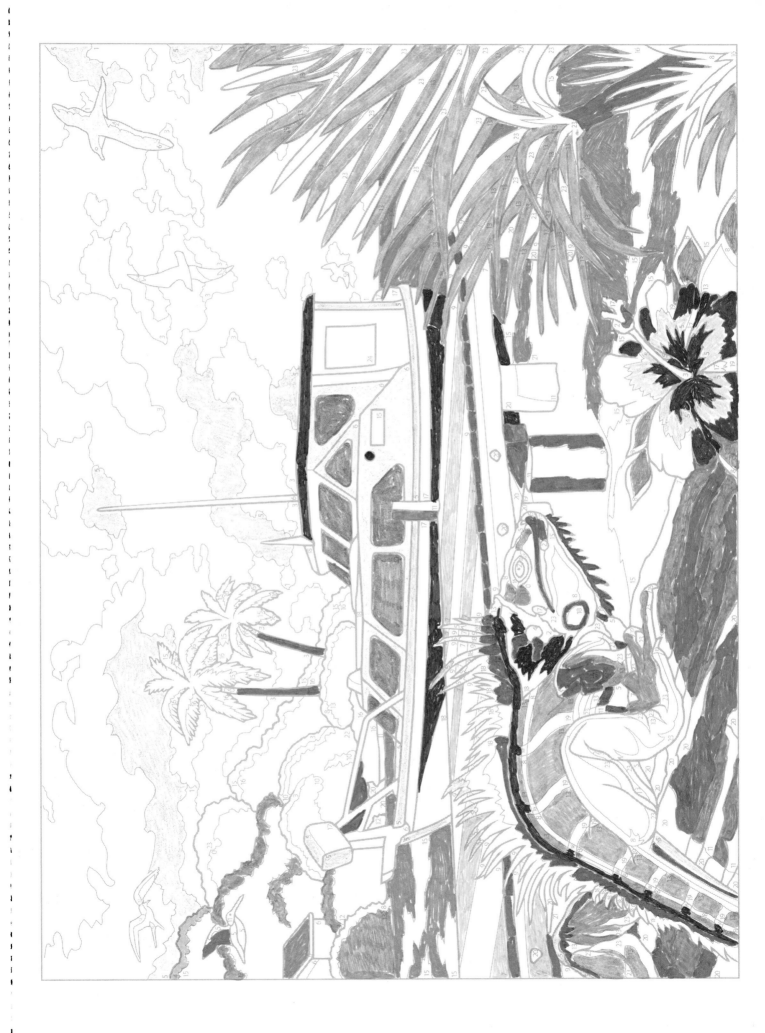

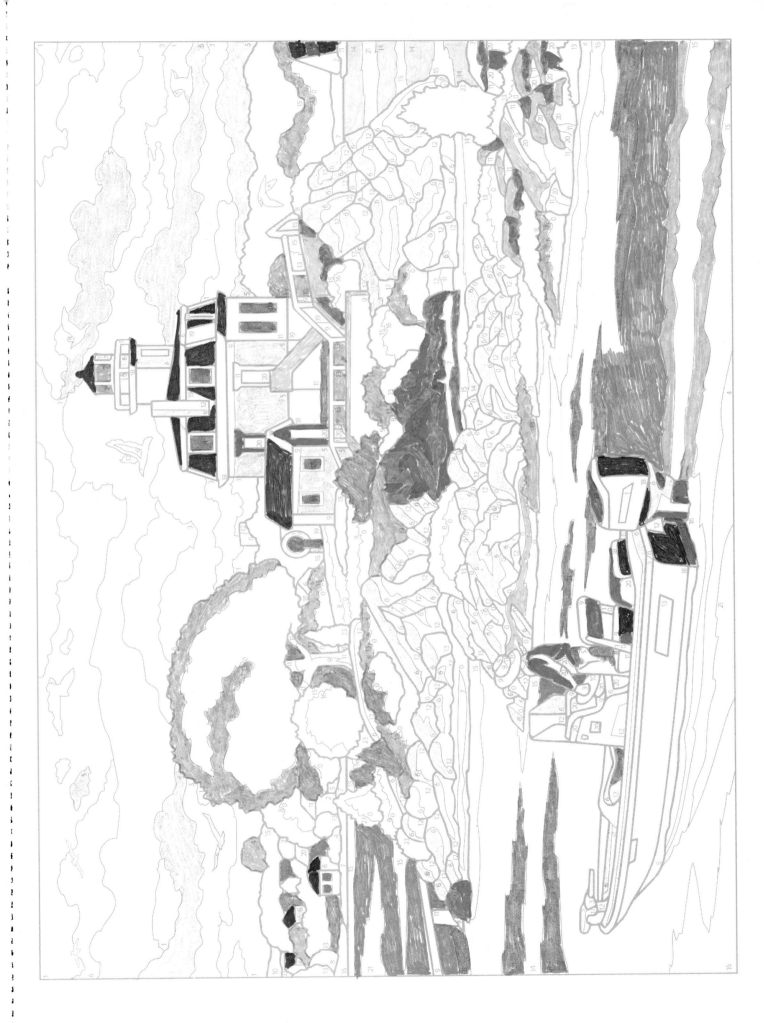

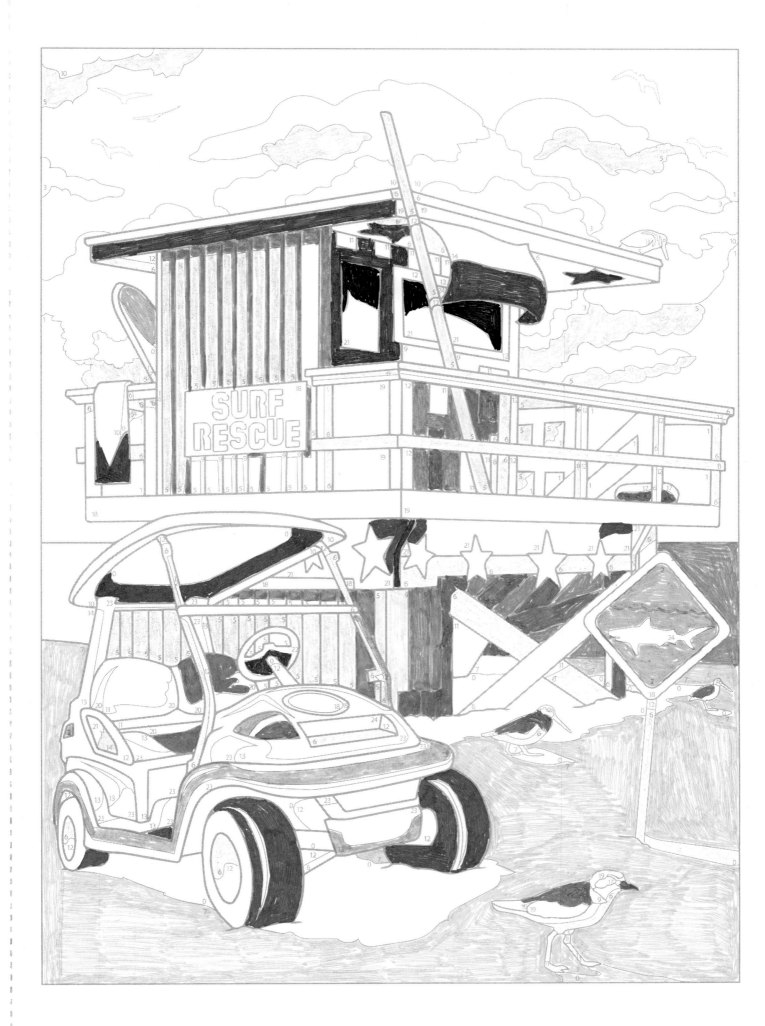

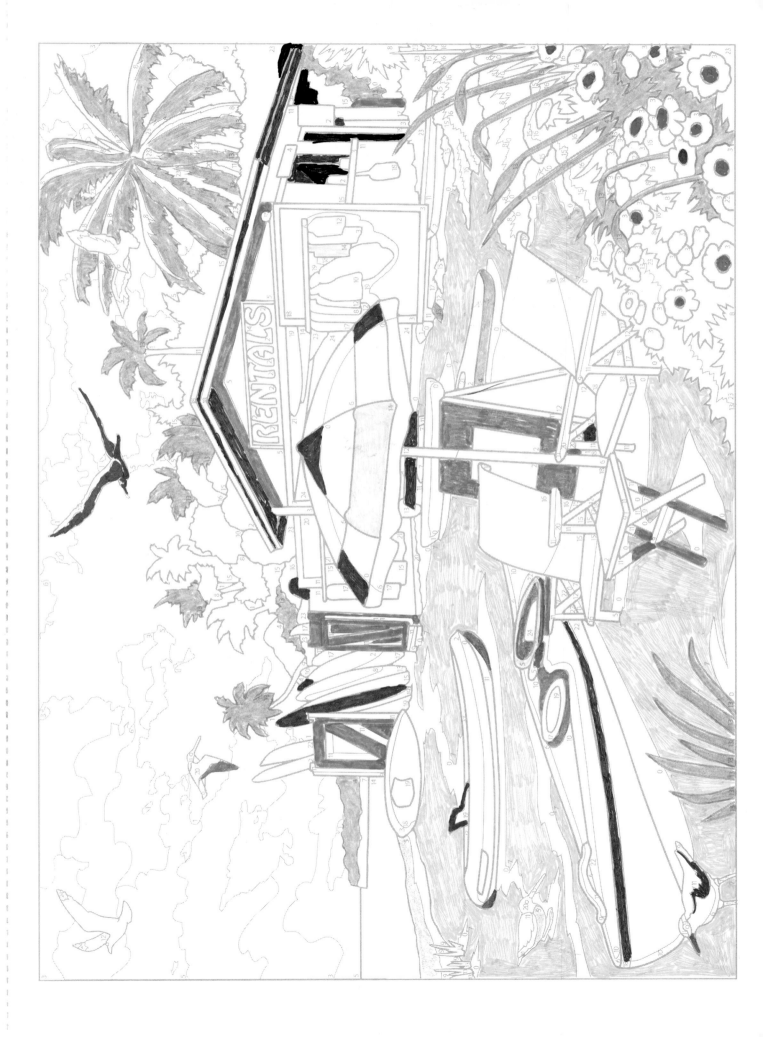

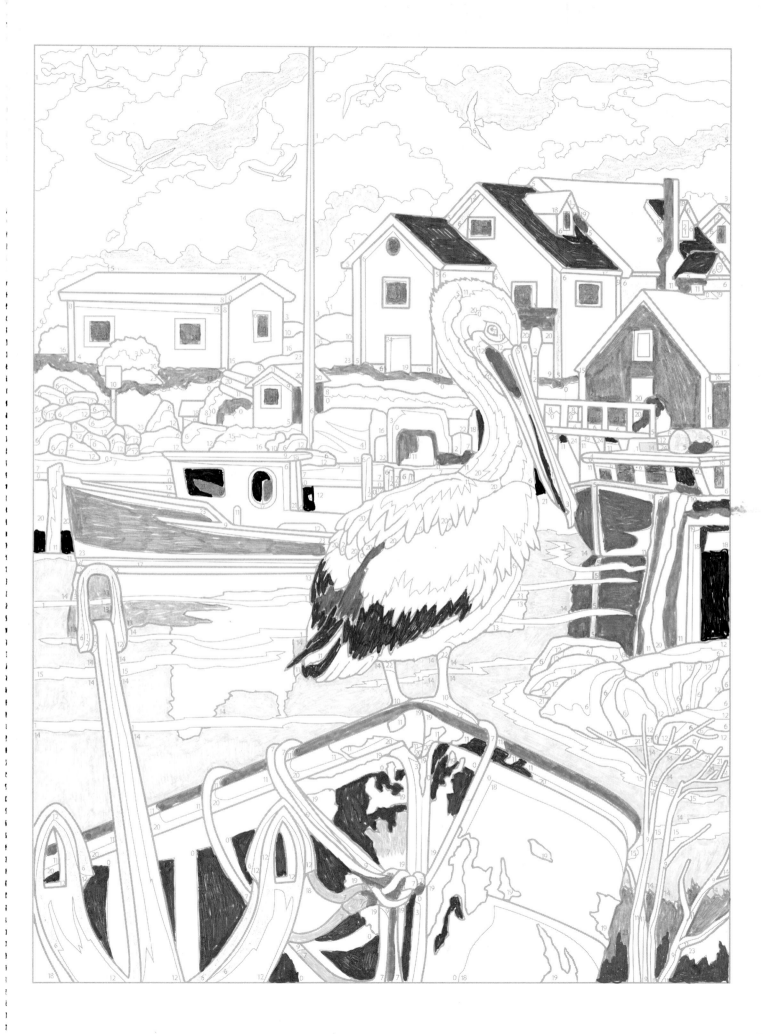